To my children and grandchildren

The Death and Resurrection of a Coherent Literature Curriculum

What Secondary English Teachers Can Do

Sandra Stotsky

ROWMAN & LITTLEFIELD EDUCATION

A division of
ROWMAN & LITTLEFIELD PUBLISHERS, INC.
Lanham • New York • Toronto • Plymouth, UK

Published in the United States of America
by Rowman & Littlefield Publishers, Inc.
A wholly owned subsidiary of The Rowman & Littlefield Publishing Group, Inc.
4501 Forbes Boulevard, Suite 200, Lanham, Maryland 20706
www.rowmanlittlefield.com

10 Thornbury Road, Plymouth PL6 7PP, United Kingdom

British Library Cataloguing in Publication Information Available

Library of Congress Cataloging-in-Publication Data

Stotsky, Sandra.
  The death and resurrection of a coherent literature curriculum : what
secondary English teachers can do / Sandra Stotsky.
      p. cm.
  Includes bibliographical references.
  ISBN 978-1-61048-557-9 (cloth : alk. paper) — ISBN 978-1-61048-558-6
(pbk. : alk. paper) — ISBN 978-1-61048-559-3 (electronic)
  1. Reading (Secondary)—United States. 2. Literature—Study and teaching
(Secondary—United States. 3. Literature—History and criticism—Theory,
etc—Study and teaching (Secondary) I. Title.
  LB1632.S85 2012
  807.1'273—dc23
                                                              2012010463

∞™ The paper used in this publication meets the minimum requirements of
American National Standard for Information Sciences—Permanence of
Paper for Printed Library Materials, ANSI/NISO Z39.48-1992.

Printed in the United States of America

Contents

List of Tables   ix

Preface   xi

Introduction   xiii

1   What Reading Programs for Incoming College
Freshmen Imply   1
    Why Colleges Sponsor Reading Programs for
       Incoming College Freshmen   2
    Highlights of the 2011 Beach Book Report   3
       Criteria Used by Selection Committees   4
       Reading Levels   6
       What the Reading Levels Imply   8
       Issues in Current Selection Criteria   9

2   What the 2010 National Literature Survey Found   15
    Evidence for a Plateau or Decline   16
    Questions Guiding the Survey   19
    Content and Instruction in Secondary Literature Classes   20
    Teachers in the Survey and their Characteristics   21
    The Readability Formula Used   22
    Survey Results   23
       Major Titles Assigned   23

Level of Reading Difficulty from Grade 9 to Grade 11   26
Anthology Use   28
Major Poets, Short Story Writers, and Nonfiction
     Authors Assigned   28
How Required Titles Are Chosen   29
How Teachers Approach Literary Study   29
Classroom Practices Surveyed   32
Time Allotted to Literary Study   33

3   The Demise of a Coherent and Demanding
Literature Curriculum   39
   Influence of the Committee of Ten   39
   Contents of a Coherent and Demanding
     Literature Curriculum   40
   Beginning Fragmentation of the Secondary
     Literature Curriculum   43

4   Abandonment of Intellectual Goals in the Literature Class   53
   New Sources of Incoherence   54
   Professional Sources of Intimidation   61

5   How NCTE Encouraged Deeper Literary Chaos   69
   The 1996 NCTE/IRA Standards   69
     How to Turn the English Class into an Ersatz Social
       Studies Class   72
     How to Turn the English Class into a Creative Arts Class   74
     Influence on State Standards   75
     Sources of Influence on the NCTE/IRA Standards   77
   Opposition to Literary Guidelines   78
   Support for Literary Guidelines   83

6   How an Incoherent Literature Curriculum Slows Down
Intellectual Development   91
   What Coherence Looks Like in a Literary Reader   91
   Effects of Incoherence on Reading Levels   93
     Easy-to-Read Contemporary Literary Texts in High School   94
     Elementary-Level Literary Texts in the Middle School   97
   Can Common Core Help?   98

7 How Two Learning Theories Further Cripple Literary Study 103

Changes in Approaches to Literary Study at the
Secondary Level 104

Two Learning Theories Driving Pedagogy in the
Literature Curriculum 105

Constructivism 106

Social Justice and Critical Pedagogy 108

How These Theories Influence Literary Study and the
School's Civic Mission 110

8 How to Create Coherent Sequences of Informational Texts 125

The State of Civic Literacy in the Schools 126

Curriculum Placement Problems 127

Common Core's Reading Standards 128

Common Core's College and Career
Readiness Standards 129

Purpose of the College and Career
Readiness Standards 130

How their Intellectual and Civic Goals Can Guide
Curriculum Developers 132

Implications for Professional Development and
Teacher Licensure 137

Implications for the High School History/U.S.
Government Curriculum 138

9 Principles for Coherent Literature Sequences 141

A Multi-Year Literature Sequence for Grade 6 to
Grade 8 142

An Intensive 14-Month Literature Sequence Beginning
in Grade 6 147

Principles for Developing Coherence and
Critical Thinking 150

Using Nonfiction to Provide the Historical and
Cultural Context for Literary Readings 151

10 Doing the "Right Thing": Comedy and Political Satire in
Grade 8 157
Jamie Highfill

The Skills-Based Curriculum in Arkansas 158
Background to a Coherent Grade 8
 Literature Curriculum 160
My Grade 8 Literature Curriculum 163
How this Curriculum Is Taught 164

11 Introducing Close Reading in High School English Classes 171
Ashley Gerhardson and Christian Goering
 Introducing Close Reading in Fort Smith, Arkansas 172
 Introducing Close Reading in Topeka, Kansas 178
 Close Reading and the Common Core 180

12 What Should English Teachers Do? 183
 Obstacles in Reconstructing Cumulative Sequences in
  Literary Study 188
 Teacher Autonomy 188
 Uncriticizable Social Goals 189
 Non-Cognitively-Oriented Pedagogies 190
 Lack of Academic and Professional Guidance 190
 What to Do? 192

About the Author 197

List of Tables

Table 2.1.   Top 40 Titles, Readability Level, and Read Count for
1500 Boys and Girls in the Top 10% of Reading
Achievement in Grades 9–12 in the 2009
Renaissance Learning Report   18

Table 2.2.   The 20 Most Frequently Assigned Titles,
Their Readability Level, Word Count, and
Grade Level Distribution, and Percentage of
Total Number of Courses   24

Table 2.3.   Percent of Teachers in 2009 Teaching the Most
Frequently Assigned Works in 1989   26

Table 2.4.   Mean Readability Level by Number of Titles
Assigned by Grade   27

Table 2.5.   Approach(es) to Teaching Imaginative Literature   29

Table 2.6.   Approach(es) to Teaching Literary Nonfiction   29

Preface

This book is addressed primarily to secondary English teachers. They are the only ones who can reconstruct a secondary literature curriculum in this country worthy of its name. It is now in shambles, but it was once something that literature professors, their students who became English teachers, and their students who also loved to read were proud of.

I had several purposes in mind in writing this book. One was to challenge English educators who discredit the assignment of difficult works to high school students. All high school graduates should be able to read demanding works of fiction and nonfiction, no matter who wrote them, and enjoy the solitary pleasure they give us. Our schools lack a challenging reading curriculum that enables all students, regardless of race, ethnicity, or parental income, to read more than "graphic" novels and to be able to think "critically."

Many English educators may believe that free choice in what to read in their literature curriculum motivates students as readers, even though nothing supports this belief. Trends in reading achievement as measured by the "nation's report card" certainly don't support this belief. Some fear that the only appropriately difficult texts they could assign would be by dreadful white males (DWMs). I have heard this fear expressed by teachers, researchers, and education school faculty as if only dead white males had ever written texts suitable for students with high school-level reading skills. It seems they would prefer illiterate students rather than students reading the books James Baldwin read in school.

Despite their opposition, the imperative to develop a progressively more challenging literature curriculum is being driven by Common Core's English language arts standards, adopted by forty-seven states as of this writing. These standards explicitly seek to upgrade the level of difficulty and complexity of what students are assigned to read in the secondary English curriculum in this country so that all will be "college or career ready." To emphasize this goal, Common Core provides an appendix with a list of titles grouped by genre at each grade level illustrating the level of reading difficulty and complexity it wants teachers to aim for at that grade level.

A second purpose for this book was to explain how we got to the point where most faculty in our schools of education—where most secondary English teachers are trained—do not realize or do not care that the secondary literature curriculum is incoherent. The topic is simply not addressed in their professional literature or in their coursework for prospective or practicing teachers. Without a coherent literature curriculum in the secondary grades, most students will remain at about the fifth or sixth grade reading level, which is where they are now according to several independent sources of information.

A third purpose for this book is to make the case for teaching students how to read analytically (and, as night follows day, how to write analytically). Ordinary citizens might be forgiven for wondering why this is a case that needs to be made. But, in the context of an educational mindset that has deemed most students as alienated and unmotivated to learn anything at all, the imperative to "engage" students in reading anything at all has trumped the academic functions English teachers have been expected to carry out. How they can restore the primacy of their academic roles is the ultimate purpose of this book.

Introduction

From the beginning of the twentieth century until the decade after World War II, it was generally accepted that literary study (which always included both imaginative literature and nonfiction in the form of biographies and well-written essays and speeches) was one of the three central components of the English curriculum. The other two were composition and language study—the conventions and appropriate, effective uses of the English language itself.

The overarching goal of our public schools was to prepare each new generation for informed, responsible, and active participation in the activities of self-government. Thus, the often explicit goal of the K–12 English curriculum was to develop the ability to read, write, and speak in ways that promoted this overarching goal.

It was also common sense that the curriculum—the sequence of topics, concepts, or texts to be taught—should be progressively more challenging in every subject, moving students from concrete, experience-based, and emotion-laden thinking to more abstract and rational thinking, with an increasing fund of information and ideas in their heads to think with.

Serious rethinking about the structure and content of the school curriculum began within a decade after World War II, much of it in response to the academic deficiencies the U.S. military had found in recruits.[1] The curricula and textbooks developed in the 1950s and 1960s, mostly as a reaction to Sputnik, beginning in mathematics and science and then spreading to English and history (unfortunately submerged in what was called social studies), aimed to strengthen the academic curriculum for all K–12 students.

But passage of the first Elementary and Secondary Education Act in 1965 turned public attention and funding away from strengthening the academic curriculum for all students to improving academic outcomes for only low-achieving students. The continuous changes in the content of the literature curriculum to this very day, all reflecting this different goal, have resulted in little improvement in the academic achievement of the lowest-achieving students in our public schools, negative consequences for the vast middle group of students, and negative implications for this country's economic future.

The initial fragmentation of coherent sequences and course structures in the secondary literature curriculum also began in the 1960s. Chiefly responsible were the conversion of the year-long high school English course into semester-long electives, and the conversion of junior high schools with a decided academic orientation into middle schools with a pronounced social orientation and, over time, with less academically qualified teachers than those in the junior high schools.

The middle school did not turn out to be the answer to the educational problems the educators perceived (too much emphasis on academic achievement). But it was clear that the varied interests of nonacademically oriented students were not being met by the structure of the junior high school or the comprehensive American high school—unique American models for secondary education developed in the nineteenth and early twentieth centuries. As long ago as 1934, a professor at Teachers College, Columbia University, Isaac Kandel, had observed that the comprehensive American high school sought to provide on "equal and identical terms all those types of education which elsewhere are distributed among a variety of schools."

The almost routine promotion of young adolescents with rudimentary reading, writing, and arithmetic skills into the secondary grades and the growing political desire to retain these youngsters through high school had occasioned most revisions of the literature curriculum. By the 1970s, it was possible to identify three different models for organizing high school English courses. In two models literary knowledge was no longer an identified goal of the secondary English class. And the secondary literature curriculum was becoming increasingly incoherent.

By the final decade of the twentieth century, encouraged by English teachers' major organization (the National Council of Teachers of English), shrunken and incoherent literature curricula were now the norm. NCTE had ensured that literary study and knowledge would no longer be a major goal of the secondary English curriculum by the national "standards" it created in 1996 and by its negative position on recommended reading lists of any kind. The changes in the content of literary study blessed by NCTE's "standards" made their own contribution to the relatively mediocre achievement of American students, as suggested by the results of international tests.

Perhaps the chief effect of the curricular and pedagogical changes made in the literature curriculum was to slow down the intellectual growth of the broad middle third of our student population in their high school years, as reflected by the numbers needing remediation as college freshmen. (The top 20 percent or so went to selective colleges that provided no remedial coursework, and the bottom 30 percent or so dropped out before grade 12.) Although ACT's 2011 report showed that only 52 percent of all ACT-tested high school graduates met its College Readiness Benchmark for Reading, a higher percentage had long been admitted to college despite their lack of readiness.

This book bounces off a survey of major works assigned in standard and honors courses by a representative sample of over four hundred high school English teachers nationwide in grades 9, 10, and 11 and the teaching approaches they use. The complete report appears as "FORUM 4," released by the Association of Literary Scholars, Critics, and Writers in Fall 2010. The results of this survey were confirmed by the results of an almost identical survey in one state—Arkansas—conducted by a different survey research center that located and interviewed a representative sample of over four hundred high school English teachers in the state.

Both surveys found that the content of the literature curriculum for students in standard or honors courses in grades 9, 10, and 11 is no longer traditional or uniform in any consistent way; that these students do not read an increasingly more challenging set of major titles from grade 9 to grade 11; and that their teachers tend to use nonanalytic approaches for the study of both imaginative literature and literary nonfiction. A dysfunctional literature curriculum in every way.

It is not clear why English teachers are under-using close reading for nonfiction and, in the short amount of time they have for teaching any component of the English language arts at the high school level, turning students' attention away from what is in a text toward material on its historical, cultural, or biographical context. Such instructional practices may well be a major contributing factor to the unsatisfactory results on tests of college readiness.

Chapter One zeroes in on the increasingly popular college-sponsored reading programs for incoming freshmen as further evidence of the deficiencies in secondary literature curricula. The low reading level of so many of the books in these reading programs in both public and private colleges indicates how much higher education has had to lower its academic standards to accommodate graduates of our dysfunctional high schools. Trustees need to decide whether the books chosen for reading programs for incoming freshmen should be selected for their potential to develop the analytical reading skills and cultural knowledge needed for real college coursework.

Chapter Two explains the origin, scope, and methodology of the 2010 national literature survey of English teachers in grades 9, 10, and 11 in public schools. Its three major results serve as the point of departure for the other chapters in the book.

Chapters Three and Four provide a history of literary study in American schools from around the turn of the twentieth century, when it was first established as one of three central components of a modern high school subject, to the 1970s, when it was possible to identify three different models for organizing high school English courses. In only one model was literary knowledge a goal of the secondary English class.

Chapter Five explains how the "standards" released by the National Council of Teachers of English and the International Reading Association in 1996, and their refusal to provide a recommended reading list to accompany these standards, prevented any possible reconstruction of a coherent secondary literature curriculum. Once the goals of the multicultural movement became almost wholly attitudinal (i.e., they were no longer attempting to broaden cultural horizons), the multicultural texts English teachers were encouraged to assign were more likely to develop emotion-laden, misinformed, and incoherent thinking than "critical thinking," another benefit that many educators had claimed for reading them.

Chapter Six suggests how an incoherent literature curriculum may influence what students read. It first describes a well-known literary reader to show what coherence means in this text. It then shows how incoherent literature curricula affected the reading level of what the broad middle third of our student population read in their literature curriculum.

Turning from curricular issues to pedagogical issues, Chapter Seven describes the two learning theories and their pedagogical counterparts dominating teacher preparation, professional development, and instruction in the secondary literature class today. It then shows their influence on the pedagogical apparatus developed by English educators for a nationally known literature anthology.

Moving from the negative to the positive, Chapter Eight shows how English teachers or curriculum developers might use Common Core's few content-rich high school English standards to stimulate a coherent sequence of informational texts over the course of the secondary grades. While Common Core's standards are not the solution to a dysfunctional literature and civics curriculum, these particular standards do provide clear intellectual and civic goals to guide the selection and sequencing of some of the literary and informational texts in the secondary literature curriculum.

Chapter Nine presents five principles that undergird coherence in a literature curriculum, whether for one grade level and/or across several grade levels. Abstracted from the literary sequences in two academically demanding private schools, one for very able girls and the other for very able minority students, these principles can be used to guide the reconstruction of coherent literature curricula in our public schools from grade 6 to grade 12.

Chapter Ten is an invited essay by a grade 8 teacher who was named Arkansas's Outstanding Middle Level Language Arts Teacher for 2011. In it, Jamie Highfill describes the classroom literature curriculum she developed to fill in the "gaps" in her students' literary and cultural knowledge, the resources she drew on to develop it, and how she teaches it. When she began teaching in a Fayetteville junior high school in 2002, she was stunned by what her students didn't know. She thought carefully about what they should know before grade 9 and gradually constructed a classroom curriculum that would fill in the gaps she perceived and prepare them for what should be even more demanding coursework in high school.

Chapter Eleven is another invited essay to address the problem many English teachers now face—how to begin to teach close reading to students whose experience in the literature class has been limited to other approaches. Ashley Gerhardson, a teacher of Advanced Placement courses in Fort Smith, Arkansas, and Christian Goering, now director of the English education program at the University of Arkansas, give us a flavor of how they sought to introduce close reading practices in two very different high school English classes.

As their classroom dialogues suggest, it will not be easy for English teachers to accustom students to looking line by line, sometimes word by word, at a text to begin to understand it and what the author has done. Because close reading has also been ignored in preparation and professional development programs for English (and reading) teachers (only Advanced Placement teachers take workshops on close reading), Goering is now working with colleagues in the English department to develop a methods course for prospective English teachers that includes close reading.

Chapter Twelve offers several suggestions on what secondary English teachers who are so minded might do to construct coherent and demanding literature curricula for all students in our public schools. It is clear that their discipline-based professional interests have not been addressed well by the professional organization that was founded in 1911 to represent them and in which they may still be the majority of members.

NOTE

1. See, for example, Mary Campbell Gallagher, "Lessons from the Sputnik-Era Curriculum Reform Movement: The Institutions We Need for Educational Reform," in *What's at Stake in the K–12 Standards Wars: A Primer for Educational Policy Makers*, ed. Sandra Stotsky (New York: Peter Lang, 2000), 281–312. See also Ralph Raimi, "Judging State Standards for K–12 Mathematics Education," in *What's at Stake in the K–12 Standards Wars: A Primer For Educational Policy Makers*, ed. Sandra Stotsky (New York: Peter Lang, 2000), 33–58.

What Reading Programs for Incoming College Freshmen Imply

College-sponsored reading programs for incoming freshmen are becoming increasingly popular. These programs warrant far more attention than they have received, in large part because of a report on the books that 245 colleges assigned for summer or fall reading in 2011–2012.[1] The report comments on the generally low level of academic challenge in the books selected to initiate high school graduates into an institution of "higher" education.

The reading level of these books suggests that most of these reading programs are not rigorously academic programs aligned with the content of first-year undergraduate courses. They are, instead, oriented to the academic level of the average college freshman. Most one-book initiatives have low academic standards in order to accommodate the low reading levels, poor reading habits, and meager cultural knowledge of incoming freshmen.

Academic standards have been lowered because of the serious deficiencies in the high school literature curriculum. How else to explain such titles in reading programs for incoming freshmen as Alexie Sherman's *The Absolutely True Diary of a Part-Time Indian*, which is described on a booklist as being for grades 7–10, or Stephen Chbosky's *The Perks of Being a Wallflower*, which has about a fifth grade reading level?

What are the sources of the problems colleges are responding to with lowered standards? One is the low reading level of what students in standards and honors courses are assigned in high school English classes, as suggested by the results of a national survey in 2010, described in Chapter Two. Another is the inappropriate way in which students are taught to read. The information gathered by this survey indicates that students in standard and honors courses in grades 9, 10, and 11 do not experience a coherent, demanding curriculum, or a curriculum that increases in reading difficulty from grade to grade or sufficient instruction in analytical reading and writing.

In the context of a national movement to make all students ready for college, at least three questions need to be addressed. Should public colleges and universities use their reading programs for incoming freshmen to address the deficiencies in high school English curricula? What would they need to do if they wanted to do so? What should their trustees do to address the weaknesses at the secondary level?

WHY COLLEGES SPONSOR READING PROGRAMS FOR INCOMING COLLEGE FRESHMEN

College websites show a variety of reasons for their summer or fall reading program for incoming freshmen. Temple University's rationale is a common one: "the goals of the project are to provide a common intellectual experience for entering students" and to "bring students, faculty and members of the Temple community together for discussion and debate." Skidmore College also wants to provide first-year students "with a common experience centered on an intellectually interesting and challenging subject."

Ashley Thorne, author of the 2011 "Beach Book" report, speculates that the absence of a core curriculum in most colleges accounts for the goal of a "common" intellectual experience in these programs. But there is no evidence as yet that these programs provide an intellectual experience (or can provide one). What may have begun as an academic effort has ended up reflecting the very problems the original programs sought to address—the inadequacies of the secondary literature curriculum.

Instructors of required freshman composition or orientation courses today find little common cultural, literary, or historical knowledge in their students, whether they were in standard or honors English classes or, for that matter, in Advanced Placement classes, whose syllabi may differ greatly from class to class even though each syllabus must be approved by the College Board. These instructors cannot hold serious discussions of a historically and culturally important idea, writer, event, or person unless they provide relevant reading material themselves.

The basic reason, made explicit by Troy University in Alabama, is the need to develop the reading skills of their incoming college freshmen. ACT's 2011 report showed that only 52 percent of all ACT-tested high school graduates met its College Readiness Benchmark for Reading.[2] In fact, improvement of reading skills was a chief purpose of the reading program for incoming freshmen at Troy University.[3]

In describing its many purposes for this reading program, Troy University wants its freshmen to know that "there are new expectations about reading, thinking, and learning which are markedly different from the expectations of high school." This university's reading program (which, like others, also wanted to give incoming freshmen a common reading experience) was designed in response to a requirement for re-accreditation by the Southern Association of Colleges and Schools that its members create and carry out a five-year plan to enhance learning at their campuses.[4] That would explain why Meredith College in Raleigh, North Carolina, created a summer reading program to "enhance the academic climate on campus."

Responding to an ACT survey in 2005–2006, 36,000 middle school, high school, and post-secondary instructors of both regular and remedial courses across the curriculum checked off their students' inability to read complex texts as their major deficiency. Based on these responses, ACT recommended that high school students be given "more opportunities to read challenging materials ... so that they are better positioned to comprehend complex texts in all subjects once they enter college or the workplace."[5] ACT should have extended this recommendation to the college committees selecting books for reading programs for incoming freshmen.

HIGHLIGHTS OF THE 2011 BEACH BOOK REPORT

The 2011 "Beach Book" report shows what 245 American colleges and universities asked their incoming freshmen to read during the summer or at the beginning of their first semester of the 2011–2012 academic year. These 245 colleges and universities were all that could be located or had up-to-date websites. However, the number of colleges and universities is large enough to provide solid information on the general features of the selected books and the criteria used for selection.

According to the report, almost 90 percent of the colleges chose books published since January 2000, and all but two books were published after 1972. Sometimes the assignment was accompanied by a comprehension test or an essay question to prompt a composition. But this was not always the case. What did tend to accompany the assignment, Thorne drily noted, was a press release announcing the college's choice, a scheduled speech by the author, and a series of events or films related to the selection. On the question of how a selection was made, the report found considerable variation in method—often a committee representing faculty and students made the selection.

What genres do the 2011 selections reflect? Of these 245 institutions of higher education, 79 assigned memoirs, 62 assigned biographies, 48 assigned fiction, 4 assigned histories, and 1 assigned a play. Ten assigned graphic novels (comic books). As the "Beach Book" report noted, the number of assigned biographies was inflated by the popularity of *The Immortal Life of Henrietta Lacks;* of the 62 biography-assigning institutions, 39 chose *Henrietta Lacks.*

The memoir genre comprised by far the greatest variety of books selected for common reading programs: 11 different biographies and 42 different memoirs. Why so many memoirs? A Brooklyn College dean was quoted as saying that memoirs are "a genre familiar to students." In other words, no "genre" challenge for memoirs.

Criteria Used by Selection Committees

One relatively common criterion, the report noted, is availability of the author for guest lectures and book-signing. Thorne inferred that colleges seek recently published books for common reading programs for varied reasons:

- They hope to invite the author to speak on campus.
- They assume current books are more accessible to students.
- They believe students will be more enthusiastic about contemporary themes.

- They want the college itself to be identified with fashionable ideas.
- They hope to pick up on the momentum of a book that is popular with the general public and trust that more students will actually read it.
- A movie version may be available or due soon.

Indeed, the availability of the author for a campus visit was a major condition for the choice of book by the University of Arkansas in Fayetteville, which selected *No Impact Man* for 2011. This is a 2009 book on a current topic of interest—sustainability—with a documentary film already based on it. According to the co-chair, a selection committee of faculty, staff, and students decided that it would "cooperate with the introduction of the new sustainability minor, and announced to the university that it would welcome suggestions for books that dealt with sustainability in some way." About thirty titles were nominated, and the selected book "seemed to please those working with the sustainability program." As for follow-up assignments, students in the freshman composition class teaching this book "are to write a substantial paper after reading the book and attending at least two events related to it."

Author availability remains a major criterion at this university. The co-chair of the selection committee listed all the criteria in a November 2011 call for book nominations for 2012:[6]

- It must be nonfiction.
- It must be relatively current—"fresh" enough so that not many readers will have already read it.
- It must be well written and be engaging to a variety of readers.
- It may be either an extended treatment by a single author or authorial team, or it may be a collection of essays by a variety of authors, but a single author is preferred.
- The author(s) must be willing to travel to northwest Arkansas to engage the university and the community in lively discussion.
- The book must be capable of raising and addressing issues that can be considered in a variety of ancillary events: panel discussions, artistic performances, film series and so on.
- Ideally, it must be available in paperback, relatively inexpensive to buy, and around (or under) three hundred pages in length.

In contrast, the criteria used by Troy University, which selected Mary Shelley's *Frankenstein* for 2010–2011, included readability and applicability to a broad group of first-year learners (traditional, non-traditional, face-to-face, and electronic students). *Frankenstein* was a better selection than the books chosen for piloting the summer reading program, for reasons noted in an independent evaluation of the framework for the program.[7] As with the pilot selections (which had included Janisse Ray's *Ecology of a Cracker Childhood* and Cormac McCarthy's *The Road*), adolescents tend to be motivated to read it (in the case of *Frankenstein* because of its plot). But its vocabulary is advanced, and it is much longer and more difficult than the pilot selections—thus a more challenging but still appropriate book for entering freshmen.

For 2011–2012, Troy University selected David Malouf's *Ransom*, a 2009 book retelling the story of *The Iliad* from Books 16 to 24. A well-known Australian novelist, short-story writer, and poet, Malouf re-imagines the circumstances leading up to the climactic scene of *The Iliad*: King Priam's visit to Achilles to beg for the body of his son Hector. According to an item on Google, *Ransom* is already studied in some Australian high schools.

Ransom seems to have been a particularly appropriate choice for a summer reading program because of the film series it generated at this university. The films included: *Troy, Clash of the Titans, 300* (a fictionalized retelling of the *Battle of Thermopylae*), *Helen of Troy, Animal House, Spartacus*, and *Hercules Unchained*. Each film in the weekly film series began with a fifteen-minute lecture by a faculty member from a different department. By the time freshmen had read and discussed the book, seen (or re-seen, as the case may well be) some of these films, and heard faculty lectures, they had likely acquired a strong knowledge of Classical Greece, some ancient history, Greek mythology, and the meaning of metaphors frequently used by modern literary and political writers of the English language.

Reading Levels

The 2011 "Beach Book" report commented on the lack of intellectual challenge in the books chosen for college reading programs as a whole, echoing the title of a 2007 essay by Anthony Paletta, "The Unseriousness of Freshman Summer Reading."[8] The readability level (RL) of a number of beach books might therefore suggest whether there was some consistency between Thorne's and Paletta's observations and the results of the 2010 high school literature survey. Are books for incoming college freshmen as relatively undemanding in reading level as the texts (as a whole) assigned by high school English teachers?

The chart below provides an initial answer. But first, a few words on the formula used to determine the level of reading difficulty for a random number of beach books. Like most readability formulas, it consists of measures of word difficulty and sentence difficulty. It also incorporates book length (number of words), an important variable not used in many readability formulas; the formula is adjusted upward for longer books and downward for shorter books.[9] Moreover, the score it produces indicates the book's grade level placement. The readability levels for many titles listed in the 2011 "Beach Book" report are not on the formula developer's website probably because its lists do not include recent books that are not in school libraries and/or are not taught in American high school English classes.[10]

Readability formulas have some limitations when applied to literary works—and these limitations have always been acknowledged by serious reading researchers.[11] Readability formulas do not work well for poetry, for example. And they cannot capture many aspects of literary complexity (e.g., theme, character motivation). They work extremely well for expository nonfiction texts. Although they are not a substitute for the professional judgment of well-read and experienced English teachers, objective measures of word and sentence difficulty are useful to researchers, given how unlikely it is to expect any group of English teachers to agree when rating the purely literary features of a literary text for their level of difficulty.

Here are the first twenty titles listed in the 2011 "Beach Book" report that could be found on the website provided by Renaissance Learning, developer of the readability formula used here:

Atwood, Margaret, *Oryx and Crake*, 6.2

Chbosky, Stephen, *The Perks of Being a Wallflower*, 4.8

Danticat, Edwidge, *Brother, I'm Dying*, 6.9

Davis, Sampson, George Jenkins, and Rameck Hunt, *The Pact*, 6.8

Dumas, Firoozeh, *Funny in Farsi: A Memoir of Growing Up Iranian in America*, 7.3

Ford, Jamie, *Hotel on the Corner of Bitter and Sweet*, 5.7

Gonzalez, Christina, *The Red Umbrella*, 3.8

Gruen, Sara, *Water for Elephants*, 4.4

Gruwell, Erin, *The Freedom Writers Diary*, 6.4

Hillenbrand, Laura, *Unbroken: A World War II Story of Survival, Resilience, and Redemption*, 7.7

Huxley, Aldous, *Brave New World*, 7.5

Kidder, Tracy, *Mountains Beyond Mountains*, 8.0

Kingsolver, Barbara, *The Bean Trees*, 5.6

Krakauer, Jon, *Into Thin Air*, 8.9

McBride, James, *The Color of Water: A Black Man's Tribute to His White Mother*, 6.1

Nazario, Sonia, *Enrique's Journey: The Story of a Boy's Dangerous Odyssey to Reunite with His Mother*, 5.6

Otsucka, Julie, *When the Emperor Was Divine*, 5.0

Sherman, Alexie, *The Absolutely True Diary of a Part-Time Indian* (for grades 7–10)

Stockett, Kathryn, *The Help*, 4.4

Suskind, Ron, *A Hope in the Unseen*, 7.5

Twain, Mark, *Connecticut Yankee in King Arthur's Court*, 9.2

Welty, Eudora, *The Optimist's Daughter*, 5.6

What the Reading Levels Imply

As can be seen, almost all of these books have readability scores at a lower middle school level (grades 4, 5, and 6). Only a few are at a higher middle school or a high school level (grades 7, 8, and higher), including the only two books written before 1972 (*Brave New World* and *Connecticut Yankee in King Arthur's Court*). All these novels and memoirs may be praiseworthy for their literary quality, and their themes, topics, or characters conceptually complex. But for most titles, their vocabulary and syntax are not a challenge for an incoming college freshman with adequate high school level reading skills.

Surely books about important ideas in the academic disciplines, written at an appropriately demanding reading level, could have been found. Instead, colleges have chosen to lower their standards or to keep them as low as the reading levels of their incoming freshmen.

If a major purpose of a college-sponsored reading program for incoming freshmen is to ease their transition to the books or textbooks they have to read in the other courses they take, or help them to gain significant cultural or literary knowledge, or serve as a means to reinforce (or introduce) analytical reading skills, it is doubtful that most of these titles can serve these broad intellectual goals. In fact, many seem to have been chosen to serve other goals, goals that do not require college-level reading skills.

Issues In Current Selection Criteria

There are many academic purposes for having a common reading selection. They include (1) giving students a common college-level reading experience for discussion in freshman classes, (2) enhancing common cultural knowledge, (3) stimulating further author- or topic-related reading, (4) learning the relevance of a book's content for related freshman coursework, (5) increasing students' focus on a text's discipline-related ideas, and (6) developing reading skills specific to the type of text chosen.

Clearly, books can be chosen that challenge incoming freshmen as readers. More important, these books can serve to develop analytical reading skills if chosen for their potential in this respect and if their freshman instructors can teach the chosen book in this way. However, it is likely that instructors of freshman classes that discuss the summer or fall book may need to be trained in close reading before they are assigned to teach freshmen how to read analytically.

The co-chair of the book selection committee at the University of Arkansas noted that "the teaching of the selected book is a major focus in a course on composition pedagogy taken by most of the teaching assistants who teach it." However, it is not clear if the focus of this course is on how to teach close reading. Trustees at any college would need further information on the courses in which selected books are discussed to determine whether they are conscientiously used to further incoming students' analytical reading skills.

How would trustees of colleges and universities with summer reading programs for incoming freshmen know if their programs are effective? They would first need to know whether the books selected for them have lent themselves to teaching college instructors how to teach analytical reading or to teaching freshmen how to read analytically. So far, there is no information on how well the books selected in the past three years either at the University of Arkansas (*The Devil's Highway, The Immortal Life of Henrietta Lacks,* and *No Impact Man*) or at Troy University (*Ecology of a Cracker Childhood, Frankenstein,* and *Ransom*)—or anywhere else—have served these purposes. Without this information and without systematic assessments, trustees cannot learn whether reading programs for incoming freshmen serve academic purposes and to what extent.

Troy University commendably set forth a number of indices by which it would assess its new extra-curricular reading program before implementing it. Because it wanted, among other objectives, to improve "the culture of reading" on all its campuses, it set forth such broad goals as "greater discernment and critical/analytical judgment," "enhanced writing skills," and "greater understanding of the connections among and between reading materials."

It then set forth a variety of indices that could show improvement, such as information from surveys of freshmen, graduating seniors, and participating faculty, measures of academic proficiency and progress, and attendance at complementary events. So far, however, there is no information available on what freshmen have gained from their summer or fall reading programs at any higher education institution.

Given the large number of students placed in "developmental" reading classes in their freshman year, it would seem that the criteria for book selection should be changed by public colleges and universities to help them to better achieve their own academic purposes. Most of the current programs are testimony to the deficiencies in the secondary literature curriculum. Too many of the books seem to be oriented to activities to promote an author or a political or social cause as ways to accommodate low reading skills.

For example, the office for campus sustainability at the University of Arkansas is sponsoring and organizing an event called the "No Impact Competition" in 2011–2012. According to the press release, "the competition enables people to measure their environmental and social impacts by calculating their everyday activities. It also offers ways to reduce that impact through credits or offsets that help the environment and community." But if more freshmen had experienced stronger reading programs, the office for campus sustainability could have assigned challenging books on the environment suitable for college coursework such as John Muir's and Gifford Pinchot's writings rather than a physical form of "busywork."

A different issue is raised by the selection committee's choice of Economics and Contemporary Life for its theme for 2012–2013. The call for book nominations explained:

> We were looking for a theme that would be relevant in the presidential election year, without being partisan or even overly political....We believe the economy will be a major focus of the election campaigns. Many of our students will be voting in a presidential election for the first time, and we are looking for a book that will help them understand this important issue and make an informed decision, based on facts, not rhetoric.

Regardless of the book chosen, how will composition instructors (most of whom are unlikely to have a background in economics) know what are economics facts as opposed to faulty economic thinking by the author?

CONCLUDING REMARKS

This chapter was sparked by three questions. Should public colleges and universities use summer/fall reading programs for incoming freshmen to address the deficiencies in high school English curricula? What would they need to do if they wanted to do so? What should their trustees do to address the weaknesses at the secondary level?

To judge by the titles assigned in 2011–2012 for which readability scores were available, college-sponsored reading programs do not, overall, provide a reading challenge to incoming freshmen with high school-level reading skills, never mind advanced reading skills. They don't aim higher than what the average freshman had likely read in high school.

Trustees of public undergraduate colleges should try to make their reading program for incoming freshmen better serve their own academic purposes. But they also have a responsibility to communicate to the board of education, superintendents, and high school principals in their state about the glaring weaknesses in their secondary literature programs. Since the overarching purpose of the K–12 standards their state boards of education have adopted is to make all students college ready, trustees need to let those responsible for preparing students for college know that college-sponsored reading programs should not be expected to take up the slack.

To do so as a matter of policy, they should first ask book selection committees to make the following changes in criteria:

(1) Eliminate the requirement that the book's author must be alive and able to give a guest lecture or a book signing. This one criterion drastically limits the titles that can be considered. What has far more academic relevance (if the purpose of the college-sponsored reading program is academic) is to require a work of historical nonfiction or science on a broad or general topic that has attracted sound scholarship and invite a recognized scholar on the topic to speak. This could be done with a novel, play, or long poem as well.

(2) Choose a college-level work of historical nonfiction, though not autobiography or memoir. It is rare for high school teachers of English or history to assign a complete work of historical nonfiction for students to read, as Will Fitzhugh, editor of *The Concord Review*, found in his many conversations with these teachers across the country.[12]

(3) Choose a book that looks like college-level reading, warrants close reading, and serves as a model of good English prose. It should also arouse high school graduates' interest in a college-level topic or issue in one of the academic disciplines they will study. High school students need to be challenged to read something that advances their academic vocabulary and requires more intellectual effort than the texts they read in high school. One can only applaud Troy University's goal to show its freshmen that "there are new expectations about reading, thinking, and learning which are markedly different from the expectations of high school."

(4) Consult such outside sources as the National Endowment for the Arts program "The Big Read" or the National Association of Scholars' lists. As another possibility, Ashley Thorne suggests asking alumni "Which book that you read in college influenced you the most?" and considering their answers as candidates for common reading.

Trustees should then ask their college English and history faculty to collaborate with them in drawing up a recommended reading list for high school juniors and seniors in their state. Both the faculty and the trustees also need to spell out in general terms what literary and cultural knowledge incoming freshmen should have to be ready for college-level coursework.

POINTS TO REMEMBER

1. Colleges use a variety of criteria for selecting a book for a summer or fall reading program for incoming freshmen. To judge by the readability score of a number of such books, many of those chosen for 2011–2012 cannot provide the level of reading difficulty students will find in real college reading assignments. Many also do not seem to serve as a suitable vehicle for teaching close reading.

2. The criterion that the book's author must be alive and able to appear at a book signing seems to prevent selection of a literary work or a work of historical nonfiction or science that has attracted sound scholarly criticism. This criterion should be eliminated. Students need to be introduced to models of academic argument about a book, whether or not it is hot off the press.

3. The low reading levels of the books selected for summer/fall programs for incoming freshmen point to the deficiencies of our high school literature programs. Trustees of public and private colleges need their English and history faculty to collaborate with them in drawing up a recommended reading list for high school juniors and seniors, as well as a general description of the literary and cultural knowledge they want incoming freshmen to have acquired. How these deficiencies developed and how they can be addressed are the subject of the following chapters.

NOTES

1. Ashley Thorne, Beach Books: What Do Colleges and Universities Want Students to Read Outside Class? 2011–2012, a report by the National Association of Scholars, September 2011.

2. ACT, The Condition of College and Career Readiness 2011 (Iowa City, IA: ACT, 2011). http://www.act.org/research/policymakers/cccr11/readiness1.html.

3. Creating a Culture of Reading: Troy University Quality Enhancement Plan, Revised 2009, prepared for the on-site review by the Commission on Colleges Southern Association of Colleges and Schools, April 21–23, 2009, http://sacs .troy.edu/qep/TROY-Quality-Enhancement-Plan-Revised-2009.pdf.

4. Southern Association of Colleges and Schools Commission on Colleges, "The Quality Enhancement Plan, 2008," http://www.sacscoc.org/pdf/081705/QEP%20Handbook.pdf.

5. ACT, "Aligning Postsecondary Expectations and High School Practice: The Gap Defined," Policy Implications of the ACT National Curriculum Survey® Results 2005–2006. (Iowa City, IA: ACT, 2007).

6. "One Book, One Community Committee Seeks Nominations for 2012," November 30, 2011. http://newswire.uark.edu/article.aspx?id=17314.

7. Sandra Stotsky, "Baseline Assessment of Troy University's Quality Enhancement Plan," unpublished report submitted in January 2011.

8. Anthony Paletta, "The Unseriousness of Freshman Summer Reading," *Minding the Campus*, New York: Manhattan Institute, September 20, 2007.

9. For a technical explanation of the readability formula called ATOS for Books, see Michael Milone, *The Development of ATOS: The Renaissance Readability Formula*, a 2008 report available from Renaissance Learning.

10. http://www.arbookfind.com/Default.aspx.

11. Jeanne S. Chall, Glenda Bissex, Susan S. Conrad, and Susan Harris-Sharples, *Qualitative Assessment of Text Difficulty: A Practical Guide for Teachers and Writers* (Cambridge, MA: Brookline Books, 1996).

12. http://www.tcr.org/tcr/institute.htm.

2

What the 2010 National Literature Survey Found

According to national assessments, the reading skills of American high school students have shown little or no improvement in several decades despite substantial increases over the years in funds for elementary and secondary education by state governments and Congress. Although many factors have contributed to this situation (such as demographic changes in the student body), one influence on reading achievement has been largely overlooked by education researchers—the literature and reading curriculum in secondary English classrooms.

In 2010, the Association of Literary Scholars, Critics, and Writers published the report of a survey of a nationally representative sample of over four hundred English teachers in public schools in grades 9, 10, and 11. The survey sought to find out what major titles they assign in standard and honors courses and what approaches they use for literary study.[1] Excluded from the survey were elective courses, basic and remedial courses, as well as Advanced Placement (AP), International Baccalaureate, and other advanced courses because the primary purpose of the survey was to gather information on what was happening to the broad middle third of American high school students. This chapter explains the rationale, methodology, and major findings of this survey.

EVIDENCE FOR A PLATEAU OR DECLINE

Evidence for a nationwide decline in reading achievement in this country comes from at least three major sources: an assessment of adult literacy, the nation's "Report Card" for grade 12, and the striking dip in SAT verbal (and mathematics) scores decades ago. Each source fills in the overall picture in an unexpected way.

According to the last assessment of adult literacy in this country, the reading skills of American adults declined dramatically from 1992 to 2003.[2] Moreover, the higher the educational level, the bigger the decline in the ability to read ordinary prose, one of the three kinds of literacy assessed. High school graduates declined six points on average, college graduates eleven points, and those with graduate study or graduate degrees thirteen points. The assessment wasn't trying to measure how well Americans read *Great Expectations* or *Native Son*, but merely how well adults read basic instructions and do such tasks as comparing viewpoints in two editorials.

In tandem with this decline, a report by the National Endowment for the Arts (NEA) found major declines in voluntary literary reading for both men and women between 1992 and 2002, although at different rates.[3] While a follow-up survey showed a gain in the reading of novels, the reading of books continued to slide, as did the reading of drama and poetry.

Results on the main test of grade 12 reading by the National Assessment of Educational Progress (NAEP) in 2005 also showed a decline in reading skills since 1992, when the main tests began.[4] Although both boys and girls showed a decline, there was over one grade-level difference between them in favor of the girls.

The most noteworthy decline took place decades ago. By 2012, the nosedive that the Scholastic Aptitude Test (SAT) scores took in the 1960s has long been forgotten. But this still unexplained fall not only led to the establishment of the NAEP in the late 1960s but lasted through the early 1990s.[5] The excuse that the fall was due to an increase in the number of low-income students taking the SATs was shown to be inadequate many years ago.[6] While math scores have been steadily moving back up since the early 1990s, verbal scores have not.

The trends in American College Testing (ACT) scores have corroborated the trends shown by SAT scores. According to the president of ACT,

"From the 1960s through the '80s, the national average score fluctuated constantly. Decreases outnumbered increases, and increases were seldom consecutive."[7] In addition, ACT scores for English and reading remained flat from 2000 to 2010.[8]

One possible cause of the plateau may be what many secondary students are currently reading and the difficulty level of what they read. According to a 2009 report by Renaissance Learning, a company that produces a computerized database to keep track of what K–12 students read in participating schools across the country, contemporary young adult fantasy series (by Stephenie Meyer and J. K. Rowling in particular) are among the most widely read books by secondary school students (see Table 2.1).[9]

In fact, contemporary young adult fantasies comprise ten of the top sixteen most frequently read books by the top 10 percent of high school students in 2008–2009, according to the 2009 report. The report does not indicate whether the books students read were assigned or self-selected (e.g., for book reports), but it is easy to identify those likely assigned by English teachers—such titles as *To Kill a Mockingbird, Night, Of Mice and Men,* and *The Kite Runner.* The column headed by Read Count, which tells us how many students read the book, clearly suggests that high school students going on to college have had few common reading experiences aside from this one genre—contemporary young adult fantasies. Moreover, almost all the books they read are relatively easy to read with respect to vocabulary and sentence structure.

This is the other striking feature of the top forty titles—their difficulty level. Most titles are at the middle school level, according to the readability formula used by Renaissance Learning. Few (e.g., *The Scarlet Letter, Pride and Prejudice,* and *Frankenstein*) reach the high school level of difficulty with respect to sentence structure and vocabulary. There are a few nonfiction titles mentioned, all autobiographies. The content of what students choose to read raises questions about the quality and rigor of the literature curriculum in our public schools. It does not seem that the challenges and pleasures of reading mature works are being cultivated. Nor are advanced reading skills being developed.

ACT points to a major source of the decline.[10] In a survey of almost 36,000 middle school, high school, and post-secondary instructors of both regular and remedial courses across the curriculum, ACT found students'

Table 2.1. Top 40 Titles, Readability Level, and Read Count for 1500 Boys and Girls in the Top 10% of Reading Achievement in Grades 9–12 in the 2009 Renaissance Learning Report

Rank	Grade	Read Count	Title, Author, and Readability Level
1	9–12	332	*Twilight*, Stephenie Meyer (4.9)
2	9–12	325	*Breaking Dawn*, Stephenie Meyer (4.8)
3	9–12	253	*New Moon*, Stephenie Meyer (4.7)
4	9–12	228	*Eclipse*, Stephenie Meyer (4.5, UG)
5	9–12	206	*Brisingr*, Christopher Paolini (7.8)
6	9–12	116	*To Kill a Mockingbird*, Harper Lee (5.6)
7	9–12	102	*Night*, Elie Wiesel (4.8)
8	9–12	99	*Harry Potter and the Deathly Hallows*, J. K. Rowling (6.9)
9	9–12	85	*Of Mice and Men*, John Steinbeck (4.5)
10	9–12	75	*Eldest*, Christopher Paolini (7)
11	9–12	75	*The Great Gatsby*, F. Scott Fitzgerald (7.3)
12	9–12	74	*The Host*, Stephenie Meyer (4.5)
13	9–12	74	*Fahrenheit 451*, Ray Bradbury (5.2)
14	9–12	68	*Eragon*, Christopher Paolini (5.6)
15	9–12	62	*The Kite Runner*, Khaled Hosseini (5.2)
16	9–12	62	*Harry Potter and the Half-Blood Prince*, J. K. Rowling (7.2)
17	9–12	61	*Animal Farm*, George Orwell (7.3)
18	9–12	59	*1984*, George Orwell (8.9)
19	9–12	58	*The Crucible*, Arthur Miller (4.9)
20	9–12	52	*Lord of the Flies*, William Golding (5)
21	9–12	52	*Frankenstein*, Mary Shelley (12.4)
22	9–12	49	*The Catcher in the Rye*, J. D. Salinger (4.7)
23	9–12	44	*Harry Potter and the Goblet of Fire*, J. K. Rowling (6.8)
24	9–12	43	*Harry Potter and the Chamber of Secrets*, J. K. Rowling (6.7)
25	9–12	42	*The Giver*, Lois Lowry (5.7)
26	9–12	42	*Ender's Game*, Orson Scott Card (5.5)
27	9–12	41	*Harry Potter and the Order of the Phoenix*, J. K. Rowling (7.2)
28	9–12	41	*A Separate Peace*, John Knowles (6.9)
29	9–12	40	*Pretties*, Scott Westerfeld (5.7)
30	9–12	40	*The Book Thief*, Markus Zusak (5.1)
31	9–12	40	*The Scarlet Letter* (Unabridged), Nathaniel Hawthorne (11.7)
32	9–12	39	*The Hobbit*, J. R. R. Tolkien (6.6)
33	9–12	37	*The Lightning Thief*, Rick Riordan (4.7)
34	9–12	37	*Harry Potter and the Sorcerer's Stone*, J. K. Rowling (5.5)
35	9–12	37	*The Adventures of Huckleberry Finn* (Unabridged), Mark Twain (6.6)
36	9–12	36	*Pride and Prejudice* (Unabridged), Jane Austen (12)
37	9–12	33	*Angels and Demons*, Dan Brown (5.6)
38	9–12	33	*Romeo and Juliet*, William Shakespeare (8.6)
39	9–12	33	*Uglies*, Scott Westerfeld (5.2)
40	9–12	32	*The Sea of Monsters*, Rick Riordan (4.6)

inability to read complex texts noted as their major deficiency. ACT concluded that students do not receive adequate instruction in how to read more difficult and complex works in high school and, based on that conclusion, recommended that students be given more instruction in using comprehension strategies to address this deficiency.[11]

Puzzlingly, ACT just assumed that high school students need more instruction in skills or strategies for reading complex texts—in addition to "more opportunities to read challenging materials"—in order to be ready for entry-level college coursework. However, nothing in ACT's survey (or in research studies) actually led to the conclusion that more instruction in reading strategies or skills was the chief solution to the deficiency highlighted by college instructors.

ACT could just as easily have conjectured that current teaching methods and ideas about the nature of a reading curriculum were contributing to poor reading skills. With a logical leap, it could then have hypothesized that different teaching methods and ideas about the content of an English curriculum might be more fruitful than current methods and ideas. But it didn't.

QUESTIONS GUIDING THE SURVEY

While the Renaissance Learning report tells us what thousands of high school students across the country claim to be reading (based on a short quiz about the book), it doesn't tell us what English teachers are assigning from grade to grade. Nor does it indicate how they approach literary study. So, the two overarching questions for the survey were: (1) What book-length works of fiction, poetry, drama, and nonfiction do public school English teachers assign in standard or honors courses in grades 9, 10, and 11? (2) What approach(es) do teachers use for literary study and about how much time do they allow for it? Responses to the first question would be a key to understanding whether there is a real literature curriculum in place. That is, a planned course of study requiring students to read progressively more challenging works across grade levels in ways that cumulatively build their understanding of literature, literary history, and the English language.

CONTENT AND INSTRUCTION IN
SECONDARY LITERATURE CLASSES

The last published report on the content of the secondary literature curriculum appeared a long time ago—in a 1993 volume issued by the National Council of Teachers of English (NCTE). Arthur Applebee, author
of the report, sought to find out what full-length works were assigned in
secondary English classes (grades 7–12) in a national sample of 322 public schools in 1989.[12] His study replicated a much earlier study that had
found that the most frequently assigned works then were long recognized
works of literature spanning centuries of British and American literature.[13]

One of Applebee's purposes was to determine the extent to which works
assigned in 1989 came from what he called a "white, male, Anglo-Saxon
tradition." He also wanted to find out if assigned works "adequately reflected the diversity of American culture" as well as gave students a
sense of a common cultural heritage. Although he found many changes in
what students were assigned to read over the course of the last half of the
twentieth century, he did not deem the changes "sufficient to reflect the
multicultural heritage of the United States." However, his report did not
suggest how sufficiency can be judged. Nor did it supply an example of a
curriculum that reflected this country's "multicultural heritage."

The first comprehensive report on the pedagogy for literary study in
high school English in this country appeared in a NCTE publication in
1968. James Squire and Roger Applebee's five-year study examined "outstanding" English programs through classroom observations, individual
interviews, group meetings with teachers and students, and the use of
checklists and questionnaires.[14] Altogether, 158 schools, 1,331 teachers,
and 13,291 students participated in the study. Among their many observations, Squire and Applebee found a strong emphasis on the close reading
of texts in the literature classroom. They also found 52 percent of instructional time dedicated to literary study.

Arthur Applebee also reported on the pedagogy for literary study and
the time allotted for it in his 1993 report. In a summary he noted: "teachers
reported a dual emphasis on techniques loosely related to reader-response
theories, and on those associated more directly with New Critical close
analyses of text." Interestingly, he further noted that teachers "did not see
these emphases as being in conflict with one another." A table in his report

shows that 67 percent of the public school teachers in his survey highly rated a reader response approach stressing student interpretations, while 50 percent highly rated an approach stressing a close reading of the text. He commented further:

> The eclectic melding of reader- and text-centered traditions that was apparent in teachers' goals and approaches raises a variety of questions about the consistency and coherence of the approaches teachers are adopting. . . . there are fundamental differences in criteria for adequacy of response and interpretation, in the role of historical and inter-textual knowledge, and in what is considered of primary and of secondary importance in discourse about literature (p. 137).

Applebee concluded that a "re-examination of literature curriculum and instruction is necessary to provide teachers with a unifying framework that will better inform their decisions about what and how they teach." But what he means by a "unifying framework" is not clear, nor has he yet presented one to the field.

In 2008–2009, the Department of Education Reform at the University of Arkansas sponsored a survey of over 400 English teachers of standard and honors courses in grades 9, 10, and 11 in Arkansas's public schools. The questions on the survey were similar to those in the national study.[15] The Arkansas survey was followed up by eight focus group meetings for English teachers in the state's four Congressional districts. The results of the Arkansas survey were almost identical to the results of the national study, helping to validate them.

TEACHERS IN THE SURVEY AND THEIR CHARACTERISTICS

The database used for selecting a nationally representative sample of teachers for the national study included all public schools in the United States containing grades 7–12, 9–12, 10–12, and grade 9 only (but not alternative schools and public charter schools, or private schools and Catholic schools). Public schools with fewer than one hundred students were also excluded. All records from Arkansas in the sample database were excluded to avoid contact with teachers being surveyed for the Arkansas study.

Schools were assigned to one of the nine divisions used by the U.S. Census Bureau, and a sample was selected proportionate to the number of schools in each division. The percentage and number of responding schools and the percentage and number of students in the responding schools in each census division were proportionate to the total percentage and number of schools and students in each division. Teachers were then randomly selected from the schools. Thus, the teachers and schools in this survey can be considered a representative sample of the total number of teachers and schools in this country.

Here are the important characteristics of the over four hundred English teachers in the national survey.[16] About 54 percent have been teaching English in grades 9, 10, and 11 for eleven years or more. Almost 79 percent have a bachelor's degree in English or literature. Only 36 percent indicated they had a master's degree in English or in the Arts and Sciences. Another 28 percent had a different kind of master's degree, and the others had no master's degree. This means that, unlike their counterparts in many other countries, the vast majority of the nation's English teachers do not have a master's degree in the language and literature they teach.

In response to whether they teach only English courses or other subjects as well, 65 percent indicated they teach only English or literature, while 35 percent said they teach other subjects as well. About 43 percent are fifty years old or older, and 73 percent are female. Together, the teachers described 773 different English courses, or classes: 237 grade 9 classes, 265 grade 10 classes, and 271 grade 11 classes; 78 percent described a standard course, and 22 percent described an honors course. Almost 66 percent teach twenty-five or fewer students per class.

THE READABILITY FORMULA USED

The formula developed by Renaissance Learning was used to determine the readability level of the major titles teachers mentioned. Like most readability formulas, it consists of a measure of word difficulty and a measure of sentence difficulty, and makes an adjustment for book length (number of words).[17] Most important for research purposes, the score it produces indicates a grade level placement for a text.

Gauging the reading level—and grade level—of a literary text has always posed a challenge to publishers and researchers.[18] Readability formulas do not work well, if at all, for poetry, for example. And many aspects of literary complexity (e.g., in theme, mood, character motivation) cannot be captured at all by readability formulas. Although they are not a substitute for the professional judgment of well-read and experienced English teachers, objective measures of word and sentence difficulty are, nevertheless, useful to researchers. It may be impossible to work out objective indices of literary difficulty that secondary English teachers as a whole would agree faithfully capture thematic or other subjective aspects of difficulty or complexity.

SURVEY RESULTS

Major Titles Assigned

Table 2.2 shows the twenty most frequently assigned book-length poems and major works of fiction and drama, as well as their readability level, word count, distribution across grades 9–11, and percentage of the total number of courses.[19]

While these titles reflect many centuries, from ancient Greece to Renaissance England to contemporary America, only four have a high school readability level (i.e., are sufficiently challenging with respect to vocabulary and sentence structure for a student with high school-level reading skills): *Julius Caesar, The Odyssey, The Scarlet Letter*, and *Macbeth*.

To be sure, many more of these titles are thematically complex works of contemporary fiction or drama that are appropriate only in a high school curriculum (e.g., *Night, Fahrenheit 451, The Great Gatsby, A Raisin in the Sun*). A low readability level for a literary work doesn't necessarily mean it is appropriate for young students—or that it is inappropriate for high school students with strong reading skills. It has been commonly observed that modern plays written for mature audiences have low readability levels because they consist of informal dialogue; their characters do not tend to use complex sentence structure or difficult vocabulary.

Adding the percentages across grades 9, 10, and 11 for the top four titles, we find that by the time students in standard and honors courses go

Table 2.2. The 20 Most Frequently Assigned Titles, Their Readability Level, Word Count, and Grade Level Distribution, and Percentage of Total Number of Courses*

Title	Readability Level**	Word Count	Grade 9 (N=237)	Grade 10 (N=265)	Grade 11 (N=271)	Total	Percent of Courses (773)
Romeo and Juliet	8.6	25599	160 (67.5%)	9 (3.4%)	4 (1.5%)	173	22.38
To Kill a Mockingbird	5.6	99121	80 (33.8%)	56 (21.1%)	36 (13.3%)	172	22.25
The Crucible	4.9	35560	4 (1.7%)	24 (9.1%)	131 (48.3%)	159	20.57
Julius Caesar	10.8	27309	11 (4.6%)	109 (41.1%)	7 (2.6%)	127	16.43
Of Mice and Men	4.5	29572	33 (13.9%)	28 (10.6%)	34 (12.5%)	95	12.29
Night	4.8	28404	25 (10.5%)	45 (17.0%)	14 (5.2%)	84	10.87
The Great Gatsby	7.3	47094	2 (.8%)	4 (1.5%)	77 (28.4%)	83	10.74
Lord of the Flies	5.0	59900	20 (8.4%)	40 (15.1%)	12 (4.4%)	72	9.31
Huckleberry Finn	6.7	109571	5 (2.1%)	20 (7.5%)	44 (16.2%)	69	8.93
The Scarlet Letter	11.7	63604	1 (0.4%)	13 (4.9%)	47 (17.3%)	61	7.89
Animal Farm	7.3	29060	32 (13.5%)	17 (6.4%)	10 (3.7%)	59	7.63
The Odyssey	10.3	120133	48 (20.3%)	5 (1.9%)	3 (1.1%)	56	7.24
A Raisin in the Sun	5.5	31391	11 (4.6%)	12 (4.5%)	32 (11.8%)	55	7.12
Macbeth	10.9	19048	1 (0.4%)	17 (6.4%)	26 (9.6%)	44	5.69
Antigone	5.3	11061	1 (0.4%)	39 (14.7%)	4 (1.5%)	44	5.69
The Catcher in the Rye	4.7	73404	5 (2.1%)	12 (4.5%)	20 (7.4%)	37	4.79
A Separate Peace	6.9	56787	11 (4.6%)	22 (8.3%)	2 (0.7%)	35	4.53
Fahrenheit 451	5.2	45910	11 (4.6%)	15 (5.7%)	7 (2.6%)	33	4.27
The Pearl	7.1	25845	14 (5.9%)	10 (3.8%)	3 (1.1%)	27	3.49
Speak	4.5	46591	15 (6.3%)	6 (2.3%)	5 (1.8%)	26	3.36

*The number in the grade level columns indicates the number of times the title was mentioned at that grade level.
**The number in the Readability Level column indicates the grade at which the text can be read by the average student in that grade with respect to the difficulty of its vocabulary and syntax. For example, a Readability Level of 8.6 indicates a level of reading difficulty corresponding to grade 8 and six-tenths of the school year, i.e., the text is comprehensible (with respect to its vocabulary and syntax) by the average student in the latter half of grade 8.

into grade 12, 72 percent have read *Romeo and Juliet* (mainly in grade 9), 68 percent have read *To Kill a Mockingbird* (mainly in grades 9 and 10), 48 percent have read *Julius Caesar* (mainly in grade 10), and 59 percent have read *The Crucible* (mainly in grade 11). But one cannot discern what other titles these students have read at any of these grade levels since the percentages for most of the other works mentioned are well under 30 percent.

The last column on the right, showing that most of the twenty most frequently assigned titles appear in fewer than 10 percent of the 773 courses described in the survey, serves to confirm the conclusion that can be drawn: the majority of American students experience an idiosyncratic set of assigned readings before they graduate from high school. Low frequencies, overall and by grade level, for almost all of the titles listed suggest that little is left of a coherent literature curriculum for the average student with respect to two of its major functions—to acquaint students with the literary and civic heritage of English-speaking people and an understanding of the resources in this body of literature that speakers and writers of the English language have long drawn upon.

That significant change has taken place in just the past twenty years can be seen in Table 2.3 by looking at the percentage of the 406 teachers in the 2010 national survey teaching the ten titles most frequently assigned in a majority of the public schools that Applebee surveyed in the late 1980s. For purposes of comparison, it is important to note that his study included the different types of English classes in grades 9–12 (e.g., AP, IB, advanced, elective, and basic courses), not just standard and honors classes in grades 9–11, as in the 2010 survey. Moreover, his unit of analysis was the school, not individual courses.

Although Applebee's study showed the maximum assignment of these titles on a school-wide basis, not a profile of what the average student likely read, it seems unlikely that the large differences in percentages from 1989 to 2010 can be explained just by the differences in the unit of analysis and in the types of classes included in the surveys. In other words, it is reasonable to conclude that significant changes have taken place.

It should be noted that lists of the most frequently assigned books can be misleading. Unless the percentage of courses assigning a book is 30 to 33 percent at each grade level from 9–11, lists of the most frequently assigned books do not warrant claims about which books (if any) all or most

Table 2.3.   Percent of Teachers in 2009 Teaching the Most Frequently Assigned Works in 1989

Title	Percent of Public Schools Assigning Title in Grades 9–12 in 1989 (N = 322)*	Percent of Public School Teachers Assigning Title in Grades 9–11 in 2009 (N = 406)**
Romeo and Juliet	84	30
Macbeth	81	8
Huckleberry Finn	70	13
Julius Caesar	70	22
To Kill a Mockingbird	69	30
Scarlet Letter	62	11
Of Mice and Men	56	18
Hamlet	55	5
The Great Gatsby	54	15
Lord of the Flies	54	13

*Excerpted from Table 5.4: Most Popular Titles of Book-Length Works, Grades 9–12
Arthur Applebee, *Literature in the Secondary School*, NCTE Research Report No. 25, 1993.
**These teachers were teaching standard or honors courses only.

students end up reading by grade 12. For example, Table 2.2 shows that *The Odyssey* is the twelfth most frequently assigned title overall, but only 20 percent of students read it in grade 9, where it tends to be assigned. *The Adventures of Huckleberry Finn* is the ninth most frequently assigned title overall, but in grade 11, where it tends to be assigned, only 16 percent of the courses include it. This means that a majority of the students who have read one of these works have not read the other.

Level of Reading Difficulty from Grade 9 to Grade 11

Although Table 2.2 does not allow us to determine whether students read progressively more complex and difficult works from grades 9 to 11, information about the assigned works does allow us to say something about the level of reading difficulty, overall, of what students read from grade to grade. First, the total number of book-length poems or major works of fiction and drama assigned per grade, in the first column in Table 2.4, shows that teachers typically assigned two, three, or four novels, plays, and book-length poems in a course in 2008–2009.

Table 2.4. Mean Readability Level by Number of Titles Assigned by Grade

Number of Titles Assigned	Grade	N	Mean Readability	Minimum Readability	Maximum Readability
1	9	14	7.4143	4.5	10.3
	10	13	9.7231	4.7	10.8
	11	16	5.5625	3.5	8.5
	Total	43	7.4233	3.5	10.8
2	9	42	6.9917	3.8	10.3
	10	50	7.0560	3.1	11.1
	11	50	6.0190	3.5	10.6
	Total	142	6.6718	3.1	11.1
3	9	54	6.4741	3.8	9.5
	10	51	7.0412	3.5	10.8
	11	52	6.0718	4.3	11.5
	Total	157	6.5251	3.5	11.5
4	9	42	6.8179	4.7	8.4
	10	55	6.3645	4.7	10.8
	11	47	5.8557	4.8	8.2
	Total	144	6.3307	4.7	10.8
5	9	31	6.9001	5.0	9.3
	10	23	6.3876	4.5	7.4
	11	26	6.0249	5.0	7.8
	Total	80	6.4683	4.5	9.3
6	9	25	6.4315	5.1	8.6
	10	19	6.2646	3.6	8.0
	11	20	6.1984	5.1	8.1
	Total	64	6.3091	3.6	8.6
7 or more	9	18	6.6002	5.6	8.0
	10	30	6.7753	4.7	8.4
	11	34	6.3383	4.6	8.5
	Total	82	6.5556	4.6	8.5
Total	9	226	6.7562	3.8	10.3
	10	241	6.8778	3.1	11.1
	11	245	6.0286	3.5	11.5

Second, when we examine the mean readability level by number of assigned titles by grade for all classes, there is little difference in the mean readability level either at any one grade as the number of assigned titles increases, or from grade to grade when the same number of titles is assigned. Most mean readability levels hover around the grade 6 level. These means suggest that students in standard or honors classes are as classes not reading a more challenging group of major titles from grade to grade.

These means also suggest that most teachers of standard or honors classes in grades 9, 10, and 11 tend to balance easy and hard books in each class at all grades, no matter how many titles they assign. When they assign many titles, one may surmise it is because they need to assign easier titles to address students with lower reading skills.

Anthology Use

Between 70 and 75 percent of the teachers use an anthology, with little difference in use from grade to grade. But three-fourths say they teach fewer than half of the selections in their anthology, suggesting another possible source for incoherent literature curricula in this country. Teachers use whatever they wish to use in these anthologies, almost all of which are by major publishers of anthologies in this country.[20]

Major Poets, Short Story Writers, and Nonfiction Authors Assigned

The major poets and short story writers that teachers assign, overall and by grade level, confirm what these teachers indicated about their use of anthologies. Almost all of the poets and short story writers mentioned are in the anthologies (and have been in various editions of these anthologies for decades). The most frequently assigned short story writer is Edgar Allan Poe. The six most frequently assigned poets are Robert Frost, Emily Dickinson, Edgar Allan Poe, Langston Hughes, Walt Whitman, and William Shakespeare, in that order.

Fewer works of literary nonfiction were mentioned. Those mentioned more than fifteen times are mainly autobiographies (those by Frederick Douglass and Benjamin Franklin and Elie Wiesel's *Night*), as were many of the less frequently mentioned titles. For 341 classes, teachers mentioned no specific nonfiction title or author. Teachers also noted that much if not most of the nonfiction their students read comes from the anthologies they use; publishers have included selections or excerpts reflecting a variety of genres of literary nonfiction for many years in their anthologies, especially biographical sketches of the authors featured, as well as speeches and essays by recognized writers. The nonanthologized nonfiction that teachers assign tends to come from newspapers or magazines—again, short selections or excerpts.

Historically important speeches are taught to some extent (usually in grade 11) if a specific speech was mentioned at all. Martin Luther King Jr. is the most mentioned speech or essay writer by far, in about one-third of all classes. Abraham Lincoln is the next most assigned writer but runs a very distant second. All of the most assigned authors of essays or speeches are in the major high school anthologies.

How Required Titles Are Chosen

Between 70 and 80 percent of the teachers across grade levels select the major novels, plays, and book-length poems they assign; 30 to 40 percent are influenced by their department or school curriculum; and about 14 percent are influenced by student choice. For the most part, teachers also select the literary nonfiction and technical information they assign. The choices in the question ranged from teacher preference, department decision, and school or district curriculum to student choice.[21]

How Teachers Approach Literary Study

These two questions were of paramount interest because of external influences on the time English teachers can devote to literary study today and because of seeming contradictions among the approaches to literary study that have most influenced the preparation and professional development of English teachers for several decades. First, the approach(es) to literary study.

Before indicating what "might best describe your approach," teachers were asked to read or listen to the entire list of approaches in Tables 2.5 and 2.6: Close Reading or New Criticism, Historical or Biographical, Reader Response, Multicultural, and Something Else or Other. These

Table 2.5. Approach(es) to Teaching Imaginative Literature

Grade	Close Reading or New Criticism	Biographical or Historical	Reader Response	Multicultural	Other	Number of Classes
Grade 9	29%	19%	60%	29%	4%	228
Grade 10	31%	26%	52%	27%	3%	260
Grade 11	31%	27%	45%	27%	4%	264

Table 2.6. Approach(es) to Teaching Literary Nonfiction

Grade	Close Reading or New Criticism	Biographical or Historical	Reader Response	Multicultural	Other	Number of Classes
Grade 9	22%	37%	44%	28%	3%	185
Grade 10	22%	34%	45%	20%	4%	226
Grade 11	31%	36%	39%	21%	3%	239

categorical labels roughly reflect the dominant approaches employed or developed since study of literature became a mandated part of the secondary curriculum in the late nineteenth century.[22]

A very brief history may be useful here. From about 1880 until roughly the 1940s, a literary work was placed within a biographical/historical context and seen chiefly as an embodiment of contemporary views of literary excellence and significant ideas, with its meaning a matter of personal impression. However, according to I. A. Richards, one of the earliest and foremost critics of this approach, the traditional method of teaching "around" a work (i.e., dwelling on the author's life, milieu of the times, and political influences rather than on the work itself) left students unable to understand literature, particularly poetry, and to analyze it well.[23]

Beginning in the 1930s, becoming dominant in the 1940s, and remaining strong for three decades thereafter, an approach called "New Criticism" held sway in the teaching of literature.[24] This approach stressed analysis of the relationship between a work's form and meaning. It was described as a more "objective" criticism, focusing on the intrinsic qualities of a work rather than on its biographical or historical contexts.[25]

In the 1960s and 1970s reader response approaches gained dominance, stimulated in large part by Louise Rosenblatt's *Literature as Exploration*, first published in 1938. Even though a reader-response approach was often taken further than Rosenblatt herself intended or approved (and many varieties were developed), this family of approaches did launch the doctrine that the reader "creates the text" or "coauthors the literary work," encouraging teachers to encourage their students to ground their interpretation of a literary work in their personal experiences or idiosyncratic responses to it.[26]

In the last third of the twentieth century, approaches again came into play that sought the meaning of a literary work through its historical and cultural context, but now emphasizing the author's race, ethnicity, gender, and biography, or the experiences of the group with which an author was identified (as in a multicultural approach). Among late-twentieth-century approaches, a common thread was a general belief that the meaning of a literary work is undecidable—that its interpretation was open to a variety of possibilities.

Teachers' responses to the question about their approach to imaginative literature and literary nonfiction clearly reveal the possible incoherence in instructional approaches pointed out by Arthur Applebee in 1993. In his study, 67 percent of respondents rated very highly (on a scale from 1 to 5) the influence of "reader-centered" theories on their teaching, while 50 percent rated very highly the influence of "text-centered" theories on their teaching. On the other hand, only about 30 percent of the teachers in the 2010 survey study checked off close reading, or the careful reading of the text itself; the percentage is even smaller if one includes their preferred approach to teaching literary nonfiction.

As Table 2.5 shows, reader response, biographical, cultural, historical, or identity-based multicultural approaches dominate high school teachers' pedagogy for the study of imaginative literature. All major approaches, including close reading, are represented across classrooms, but close reading was checked off far fewer times than reader response at all three grade levels, and the percentage of classes in which a multicultural approach is used is close to the percentage of classes in which close reading is used. Indeed, much of the decrease from grade 9 to grade 11 in the percentage of classes using a reader response approach seems to be compensated for by an increase in the percentage of classes stressing biographical or historical context.

If, as Table 2.5 indicates, teachers favor nonanalytical approaches to literary study, it is possible that high school students rarely engage in close, careful reading of assigned texts as part of their classroom study. It is important to note that many teachers checked off more than one approach to show that they did not use only one approach most of the time.

Striking confirmation of the dominance of nonanalytical approaches in the study of literary texts appears in Table 2.6. The percentage of classes using close reading for literary nonfiction is almost as low as the percentage using it for imaginative literature. While the percentage using a reader-response approach is, appropriately, much lower for literary nonfiction than for imaginative literature at all grade levels, and the per-centage diminishes from grade 9 to grade 11, nevertheless, close reading is slighted at each grade level in favor of a contextual approach, if not a personal response.

Clearly, engaging students in a careful reading of a nonfiction text does not preclude asking them to locate historical, cultural, or biographi-cal information that could help them to understand it better—and helping them to determine trustworthy sources of that information. Thus it is not clear why teachers are under-using close reading for nonfiction and, in the short amount of time they have for teaching any aspect of the English language arts at the high school level, turning attention away from what is in a text and toward materials on its historical, cultural, or biographical context. In the absence of a large body of observational data on whether and how English teachers blend these different approaches, they seem to be misteaching students how to read nonfiction as well as how to under-stand an imaginative literary work.

Classroom Practices Surveyed

Almost all teachers at all grade levels organize discussion on a whole-class basis. About two-thirds use teacher-prepared questions (often provided by their literature anthologies or supplementary curriculum re-sources). However, this does not necessarily mean that discussion is part of a lecture/discussion format (a frequent interpretation of this strategy). In the Arkansas survey, teachers reported devoting a significant amount of time to reading literary texts aloud before class discussion. It is possible that reading aloud was included under the rubric of whole-class discussion by teachers in the national survey.

Reading aloud to high school students in English classes (but not the reading of poetry) is a rapidly growing phenomenon. One survey of high school teachers found that 344 of the 476 respondents read aloud to their students.[27] Respondents gave four positive reasons for reading aloud to their students: to cultivate a love of reading, to build attention to and in-terest in a topic, to model correct and fluent oral reading, and to expose students to texts otherwise unread.

It is unclear to what extent the practice of reading aloud is growing as a way to enable students who do not read outside of class or cannot read well to participate in class discussion, points brought up by Arkansas teachers in the focus groups. It is also unknown how much instructional time teachers' oral reading consumes or if this strategy discourages students in the class who would otherwise come to class prepared (i.e., having already read the text the teacher reads aloud).

About two-thirds of classes at all three grade levels also use small groups for discussion and about half of them use student-generated questions. There is no way of knowing how often small student-led discussion groups are used in standard or honors English classes today. These groups are a mandated strategy for organizing all literature discussion in low-performing schools under contract with America's Choice, a nationally prominent "turnaround" partner. It is difficult to see analytical reading taking place in student-led literature discussion groups unless some students are able to imitate what a well-trained teacher of close reading has modeled for them.

In addition, in over two-thirds of all classes, students do journal writing, often during class time. A comparison of the percentages for journal writing in the national survey with the percentages in the Arkansas survey suggests these results are valid. Many percentages for classroom practices are about the same.

However, it is not clear from the survey data exactly what kind of journal writing students are doing. Some of it may be strictly text-based, often referred to as annotating a text, a practice that can promote close reading. If in-class journal writing is in "response" journals, this practice may further reduce the amount of time available for close reading, whether teacher-led or student-practiced.

Time Allotted to Literary Study

A comparison of the amount of time teachers estimated they allotted to literary study with Squire and Applebee's 1968 estimate showed that the percentage spending 20 percent or less of their time on a book-length work increases from grade to grade—from 56 percent of grade 9 classes, to 60 percent of grade 10 classes, and to 64 percent of grade 11 classes. Similarly, those spending 10 percent or less of their time on a book-length work rises from 26 percent in grade 9 and 32 percent in grade 10 to 41 percent in grade 11.

These figures suggest a dramatic reduction in overall time allotted to literary study in comparison with the 52 percent of time in Squire and Applebee's study. How much of a reduction, though, is unclear. The survey question did not ask teachers to include time spent on short stories and poetry as well (which may have been included in the 1968 estimate). Although it is possible, it seems unlikely that adding the time allotted for short stories and poetry in 2010 would eliminate the enormous difference between 2010 and 1968 in overall time devoted to literary study.

There is also no increase in outside-of-class reading to compensate for the decreased time on book-length works over the grades. Although most teachers said they require outside reading at all grade levels (whether it is done is a different matter), the number of pages assigned per week remains constant: only 49 percent in grade 9, 54 percent in grade 10, and 52 percent in grade 11 require over 40 pages per week.

On the other hand, 60 percent of the classes at each grade level spend from nine to over twenty class periods per year on literary nonfiction, according to their teachers.[28] That seems like a high percentage. However, teachers gave information on time for literary nonfiction for only 511 classes in contrast to time for a major novel, play, or book-length poem for almost 700 classes. In contrast, the number of classes addressing technical or informational reading is small, only 237. Perhaps technical or informational texts are rarely or not assigned in most English classes.

CONCLUDING REMARKS

Three major results sum up the information in the 2010 national literature survey. (1) The literature curriculum for students in standard or honors courses in grades 9–11 is no longer traditional or uniform in any consistent way. (2) These students do not read a progressively more challenging set of major titles from grade to grade. (3) Their teachers tend to use a nonanalytic approach for the study of both imaginative literature and literary nonfiction. Subsequent chapters will suggest how these findings help to account for the slower intellectual development of the broad middle of our student population in their high school years.

POINTS TO REMEMBER

1. An idiosyncratic literature curriculum is most likely an incoherent curriculum.

2. Students who do not read progressively more difficult reading material are unlikely to expand their vocabularies and their ability to follow the meaning of a series of long and complex sentences.

3. Students who do not learn to read carefully and "between the lines" do not become "critical" readers and thinkers.

NOTES

1. Sandra Stotsky, *Literary Study in Grades 9, 10, and 11: A National Survey*, published as FORUM 4 (Boston: Association of Literary Scholars, Critics, and Writers, 2010). http://www.alscw.org/Forum4.pdf.

2. National Center for Education Statistics, National Assessment of Adult Literacy (Washington, DC: U.S. Department of Education, 2005).

3. National Endowment for the Arts (NEA), *Reading at Risk: A Survey of Literary Reading in America* (Washington, DC: U.S. Department of Education, 2004); NEA, *Reading on the Rise: A New Chapter in American Literacy* (Washington, DC: U.S. Department of Education, 2008).

4. National Assessment of Educational Progress, The Nation's Report Card, 2005 Assessment Results. http://nationsreportcard.gov/reading_math_grade12_2005/s0206.asp.

5. E. D. Hirsch, Jr., *The Making of Americans* (New Haven: Yale University Press, 2009). See the table on p. 42.

6. See, for example, Christopher Jenks, "What's Behind the Drop in Test Scores?" Working Papers, Department of Sociology, Harvard University, Cambridge, MA, 1978.

7. ACT, "National Press Release," ACT News (Iowa City, IA: ACT, 2000), http://www.act.org/news/releases/2000/08-17-00.html.

8. ACT, National Score Trends (Iowa City, IA: ACT, 2010). http://www.act.org/news/data/10/trends-text.html#six.

9. Renaissance Learning, *What Kids Are Reading: The Book-Reading Habits of Students in American Schools* (Wisconsin Rapids, WI: Renaissance Learning, 2009).

10. ACT, National Curriculum Survey 2005–2006. (Iowa City, IA: ACT, 2007).

11. ACT, "Aligning Postsecondary Expectations and High School Practice: The Gap Defined," Policy Implications of the ACT National Curriculum Survey® Results 2005–2006. (Iowa City, IA: ACT, 2007).

12. Arthur Applebee, *Literature in the Secondary School: Studies of Curriculum and Instruction in the United States*, Research Report No. 25 (Urbana, IL: National Council of Teachers of English, 1993).

13. Scarvia Anderson, *Between the Grimms and "The Group"* (Princeton, NJ: Educational Testing Service, 1964).

14. James Squire and Roger Applebee, *High School English Instruction Today: The National Study of High School English Programs* (Urbana, IL: National Council of Teachers of English, 1968).

15. Sandra Stotsky, Chris Goering, and David Jolliffe, *Literary Study in Grades 9, 10, and 11 in Arkansas*, Unpublished report, University of Arkansas, 2010. http://coehp.uark.edu/literary_study.pdf.

16. Stotsky, FORUM 4. See Appendix B for the survey instrument, Appendix C for the recruitment materials, and Appendix D for the classes taught by the English teachers.

17. Michael Milone, *The Development of ATOS: The Renaissance Readability Formula* (Wisconsin Rapids, WI: Renaissance Learning, 2008). http://doc.renlearn.com/KMNet/R004250827GJ11C4.pdf. The titles in Accelerated Reader's database and their readability level can be located at http://www.arbookfind.com/Default.aspx.

18. Jeanne S. Chall, Glenda Bissex, Susan Conrad, and Susan Harris-Sharples, *Qualitative Assessment of Text Difficulty: A Practical Guide for Teachers and Writers* (Cambridge, MA: Brookline Books, 1996).

19. See Stotsky, FORUM 4, Appendix F, for the complete list of major titles mentioned.

20. See Stotsky, FORUM 4, Tables 8, 9, and 10.

21. See Stotsky, FORUM 4, Tables 11, 12, and 13.

22. Arthur Applebee and Alan C. Purves, "Literature and the English Language Arts." In *Handbook of Curriculum Research*, ed. Philip Jackson (New York: Macmillan, 1992), 726–48.

23. I.A. Richards, *Practical Criticism* (New York: Harcourt Brace, 1929). See also J. A. Grimshaw, Jr., Review of *Robert B. Heilman: His Life in Letters*, ed. Edward Alexander, Richard Dunn, and Paul Jaussen (Seattle: University of Washington Press, 2009), *Academic Questions,* 2010, 23: 136–42.

24. For an understanding of this approach, see Cleanth Brooks, *Modern Poetry and the Tradition* (Chapel Hill, NC: University of North Carolina, 1939); Cleanth Brooks and Robert Heilman, *Understanding Drama* (New York: Henry Holt, 1948); Cleanth Brooks and Robert Penn Warren, *Understanding Poetry.*

New York: Henry Holt, 1938; and Cleanth Brooks and Robert Penn Warren, *Understanding Fiction* (New York: Appleton-Century-Crofts, 1938/1943).

25. John Crowe Ransom, *The New Criticism* (Norfolk, CT: New Directions, 1941).

26. See, for example, Louise Rosenblatt, "Continuing the Conversation: A Clarification," *Research in the Teaching of English*, 29 (1995): 349–54; Stewart Justman, "Bibliotherapy: Literature as Exploration Reconsidered," *Academic Questions,* 23 (2010): 125–35.

27. Mary Ann Zehr, "Reading Aloud to Teens Gains Favor among Teachers," *Education Week*, 2010, January 6.

28. See Stotsky, FORUM 4, Table 23.

3

The Demise of a Coherent and Demanding Literature Curriculum

Did American high school students ever experience a coherent and demanding literature curriculum? Yes, many did, from around 1900 to the immediate post-World War II years. Before then, literary study rarely had a central role in the English curriculum, and secondary students usually studied literary works or excerpts as part of lessons in reading, composition, or public speaking.[1]

Before the twentieth century, study of a literary work for its own sake tended to be accompanied by study of the history of literature, with attention paid more often to the history of the work than to the work itself. Textbooks were usually organized chronologically, with the life and works of the author first, and then long extracts or whole poems from the author's writings, together with brief literary "thought gems" to be committed to memory. Teachers consciously designed secondary literature programs to shape the moral character and cultural values of their students. Why their goals differed in the first half of the twentieth century and then why drastic changes to these goals occurred within decades after World War II are the subject of this chapter.

INFLUENCE OF THE COMMITTEE OF TEN

Literary study assumed a central role in the high school English curriculum around 1900 due to the efforts of the Committee of Ten and a companion committee, both of which were convened in the 1890s to work out a uniform set of requirements for college entrance. Their work led to the development of a set of syllabi in English and other subjects. The English syllabi combined literary study with composition and rhetoric, two subjects that had always been in the English language arts curriculum. These syllabi hastened the evolution of literary content from classical works to chiefly British literature. By including some relatively contemporary British works, these syllabi helped to establish literary study as a significant part of a modern high school subject that could satisfy college entrance requirements (as Greek, Latin, and mathematics had and continued to do). These syllabi strongly influenced the high school English curriculum for almost all students for the next half century

The Committee of Ten was on record for wanting a uniform and demanding curriculum based on these syllabi for all high school students, public or private; it saw "no excuse" for a two- or three-track system. Even though all public high school students after the turn of the century did not get to experience a completely uniform curriculum, in English or other subjects, most did experience a coherent as well as a demanding literature curriculum. The College Board English syllabi influenced all English courses in American high schools because most Americans at the time subscribed to the egalitarian thrust of the Committee of Ten's elitist philosophy—the best for all.

Secondary English teachers were explicitly encouraged by an academic and intellectual elite (the members of the Committee of Ten) to choose works for literary study based chiefly on their literary merit rather than on their capacity to develop character and desirable cultural values. This did not mean that works chosen for literary study were to be devoid of moral content or incapable of developing cultural values. It meant only that moral improvement and cultural assimilation were to be a much lower priority for English teachers than the cultivation of literary knowledge and literary taste in all students.

CONTENTS OF A COHERENT AND DEMANDING LITERATURE CURRICULUM

Despite the academic myth that public high schools in the nineteenth century served only a college-intending population, they were already very flexible institutions by 1900, as Isaac Kandel characterized them.[2] The ideal of one high school for all children in the community appealed to most Americans, despite the option of private schools for the children of wealthy or religious parents. But there were very practical reasons why the curriculum in a town's high school had to be flexible; most of its students did not graduate or go on to college.

American public high schools in the latter half of the nineteenth century usually had a college preparatory program, especially if there was no nearby private academy to which a town might send academically promising students (and tuition payments). But very few students attended a public high school at the time,[3] even fewer graduated from a public high school,[4] and very few of those who did graduate from a public or private school went to college.[5] It is not widely known that most public high schools in the nineteenth century served many students who did not intend to go to college even if they did complete high school.

The passage of compulsory school attendance laws in state after state beginning in 1852 with Massachusetts may have caused many students to stay on in school at least through the first or second high school grade. By 1900, thirty states required school attendance until age fourteen, which covered grade 8 but might mean grade 9 or 10 for many students.[6]

To address non-college-intending students' interests, small public high schools in the nineteenth century offered them many courses in a variety of subjects and had long done so. This range of courses satisfied the local community, which until well after World War II was completely responsible for its public schools and had traditionally supported an egalitarian thrust for the high school. The comprehensive high school that most students in a community attended was a "uniquely-American invention."[7] For example, to this day, some small Arkansas high schools offer almost as many courses as the number of students in them.[8] Moreover, in public high schools with fewer than one hundred students (true of over half of our public high schools in 1900), only 50 percent of their teachers were college graduates, probably limiting the range and rigor of what was taught in academic courses.[9]

In contrast, non-college-intending students in large urban high schools could usually enroll in non-college-preparatory courses as part of a commercial or vocational program, an enticement to complete high school. Moreover, as one might expect, teachers in large urban high schools were apt to be far more academically qualified than their rural colleagues.

It is clear from surveys and articles in the professional literature for English teachers that public high school students in college preparatory programs, however small their numbers, did experience the demanding literature curriculum developed to prepare students for the first College Board examinations beginning in 1901. For the first few years after 1900, students in grades 9 to 12 were expected to read *The Merchant of Venice, The Vicar of Wakefield, The Ancient Mariner, The Last of the Mohicans, Silas Marner, Macbeth,* Milton's *Lycidas,* and Burke's "Speech on Conciliation with the American Colonies," among other works.[10] Within a matter of five years, English teachers were already expanding the list of requirements to include a wide range of demanding titles.

Expecting the influence of the College Board to show itself in a narrow range of books read, especially in the upper grades, George Tanner conducted a survey of 67 high schools in the Midwest for a committee of the 1904 English Conference.[11] He was surprised to find 82 different books listed as first-year reading, 92 as second-year reading, 102 as third-year reading, and 107 as fourth-year reading. Students were not necessarily reading all the specific titles the literary experts had chosen for the first three-year cycles. Nevertheless, he reported, all the College Board-required readings for 1906–1908 and 1909–1911 were in his tables, which showed the forty most frequently assigned titles in grades 9–12. Summing up the objections and commendations the survey received, Tanner explained that a broadening of titles on the list was needed "to meet the various conditions in different schools, and the different personalities of the teachers."

Tanner's 1907 report addressed the major assigned readings in these sixty-seven high schools right after implementation of the College Board exams in 1901. At that time, the number of students in public high schools was growing almost exponentially—a reflection of the huge immigration to this country between 1880 and its entry into World War I, compulsory school attendance laws, and child labor laws. As Tanner's report implies, it was already getting difficult to teach the full complement of College Board-required works to the entire cohort of students in the upper grades even after students with low achievement or non-academic interests had dropped out.

What were new and old high schools doing to accommodate the enormous differences in reading skill among students in grade 9 or 10, yet prepare the most able students for college coursework (and retain the allegiance of local taxpayers)? Large public high schools began to offer required courses at different levels of difficulty, even within the college preparatory program itself. The year-long English course and core courses in other subjects came to be designated with status descriptors like Advanced, Honors, Standard, or Basic.

But there was no external guide for the level of difficulty of the literary content of a leveled English course, whether in a college preparatory, commercial, or vocational program, beyond what was on the College Board lists for its exams. Teachers' professional judgment was most likely the criterion. Possibly, teachers assigned fewer titles in an honors course than in an advanced course, and even fewer in a standard course, and spent more time on each book to adjust for the lower level of reading skill. Nevertheless, in light of the criticisms—and changes—made later, it seems their standards for what they assigned remained consistently high until well after 1945, with literary knowledge and taste as their goals.

BEGINNING FRAGMENTATION OF THE
SECONDARY LITERATURE CURRICULUM

Contrary to the myth of a "canon" (a never-changing group of literary works or authors taught from generation to generation), many of the titles taught in college preparatory and other English courses continuously changed over the decades. The literary traditions they reflected also began to change during the first half of the twentieth century.

In Tanner's 1907 study, almost all of the top forty titles were by British authors; only nine were by American writers. And only a few truly contemporary works were on the list, whether essays, poems, plays, or novels.

The trend toward a more American literature curriculum is discernible in the results of a prominent nationwide survey conducted in 1964 by Scarvia Anderson for Education Testing Service. Eighteen American authors are among her top forty-two titles, and many titles, regardless of origin, have adolescent or young protagonists (e.g., *Romeo and Juliet, The Adventures of Tom Sawyer, The Adventures of Huckleberry Finn, Great Expectations, To Kill a Mockingbird, The Pearl, Treasure Island, The*

Yearling, and *Johnny Tremain*), a reflection in part of the literature used in grades 7 and 8.

We also find a number of works featuring a woman as a central focus or character (e.g., *The Barretts of Wimpole Street, Evangeline, Jane Eyre, The King and I, Pride and Prejudice, She Stoops to Conquer, Pygmalion,* and *The Scarlet Letter*). Some of these works were distinctly contemporary.

Despite this inevitable cultural shift, quality and difficulty level were maintained (e.g., *The Scarlet Letter* and *Pride and Prejudice,* not among the original College Board-required titles, were no less difficult than whatever works they replaced). However, several important structural changes in the secondary English curriculum in the immediate decades after World War II affected the coherence and level of challenge of the literature curriculum. The first change was directed at the year-long English course.

Up to the 1950s, composition and literary study, which included both imaginative literature and nonfiction (chiefly in the form of essays, speeches, and biographies), had typically been integrated in year-long courses from grades 7 to 12. The study of rhetoric—a staple of nineteenth-century schooling—was no longer in the English curriculum and was often taught as part of a separate course on public speaking. As would be the case in many other ways, the secondary English curriculum reflected what had happened in college and university English departments.

American high schools had long used different organizational schemes for the year-long course to address the spread in reading skill and academic interest that grew wider from grade to grade the longer students stayed in school.[12] One scheme entailed use of different curricula (e.g., college preparatory, commercial, vocational, or general), with coursework and level of difficulty tailored to the goals of the particular curriculum. Abandoning use of formally different curricula and focusing on the subjects themselves, many large schools after World War II (e.g., Brookline High School in Massachusetts) chose to give students their choice of a leveled course in each subject. Choice enabled them to experience both less demanding and more demanding courses in one year, depending on their interest in a subject, their having met its prerequisites, and a teacher's permission in some cases.

Whether high school study was organized by individual subjects or different curricula, the literature curriculum in the year-long English course was coherent even if students in standard or honors courses were taught fewer demanding works or assigned fewer works as outside reading in comparison with what was taught and assigned in advanced courses. However, the break-up of the year-long high school English course into semester-long elective courses, beginning in the mid-1950s but accelerating in the mid-1960s, was the first of several movements breaking up the coherence of the literature curriculum.[13]

There were mixed motivations for carving up year-long high school English courses into a variety of electives. Some teachers saw the fragmentation into electives as a way to honor individual uniqueness and highlight the democratic roots of having and making choices. Most were undoubtedly seeking to arouse more interest in reading literature (the passion that had likely led them to become English majors and English teachers), in advanced students as well as in those with poor reading skills. According to surveys of reading interest, many students, good or poor readers, had long expressed dislike of the year-long English class.[14]

An expression of hostility to the very existence of advanced English courses can also be detected in the explicit rejection of the goal of the Committee of Ten—to provide all students with an equally challenging curriculum, whether college-intending or not. The anti-intellectual strain of the early progressive movement had also found cover under the mantle of freedom of choice, but its controlling tendencies were visible.

When Robert Small, a teacher educator, commented in 1972 that "after a period when the concept of scholarly training dominated the high school … a small but rapidly growing number of schools have attempted to [do] away with the rigid, uniform English curriculum and replace it with a curriculum of choice," he was in effect implying that public schools should not have high academic expectations for everyone.[15] Kandel had noted in 1934 that "development of the American high school has been dominated by the doctrine of equalitarianism,"[16] and the electives movement was but one later example of this egalitarian doctrine.

Small's charge that American high schools had long (or always) been driven by academic interests could be easily refuted, as Kandel had demonstrated, by the array of courses taught in them in the nineteenth and early twentieth centuries. However, Small's account of what was happening was accurate. Indeed, elective courses grew like Topsy in the late 1960s and throughout the 1970s. They might be organized by theme or topic (e.g., death or the individual versus society), depending on teachers' idiosyncratic interests. But even educators who favored them were willing to admit their limitations after parents and others began to call for a return to the "basics" (in the 1970s and 1980s) and the elimination of a high school English curriculum consisting wholly of electives.

In a 1986 article, educators Jean Brown and Lela Phillips noted that the call to return to the year-long course was "in part the result of the laissez-faire policy of developing elective courses in the past. Decision-making about elective courses was often seemingly random and often reflected the obscure interests of individual teachers rather than the needs of students."[17] This quotation is noteworthy in two ways. First, it suggests that English educators could recognize an incoherent and idiosyncratic curriculum when they saw one. Second, and far more important, they were able to criticize publicly what they had thought was a reform—a sign of professional maturity that is difficult to find today.

The proliferation of electives was not the only cause of the fragmentation of a coherent secondary literature curriculum. Remember that composition was one of the pillars of the year-long English class. In the 1960s and 1970s, mushrooming groups of researchers, teachers, and writers called for increased pedagogical attention to (and time on) the many steps in the process of composing a piece of writing: brainstorming ideas, drafting, revising, more revising, and editing.

Who would ever deny that most student writing needed improvement? Moreover, writing process advocates claimed that students would write more fluently and with greater interest if they drew on personal experience instead of what was in their reading material as the source of ideas for a composition. Class time was finite. In many high schools, composition teaching came to be separated from literary study or informational reading, in earlier grades as well as in high school electives, in order to give the composing process more time and attention. Separation was also justified and encouraged by James Moffett's influential writings in the 1960s, based on his teaching experience at Phillips Exeter Academy.[18]

More attention to the composing process was not unjustified. But no one could show that a stress on experience-based writing (whether or not in separate courses) and the extensive use of instructional time on the writing process, in K–8 especially, led to better writing in high school. Perhaps it reduced the amount of time teachers once spent on close reading. The question was never explored. The writing process movement may have had unintended negative effects that have yet to be teased out and examined.

In the meantime, another major structural change remains to be evaluated for its effects on academic achievement: the conversion of junior high schools to middle schools.[19] Junior high schools themselves had been an innovation in the early decades of the twentieth century, transforming elementary schools with eight grades and high schools with four—or secondary schools with grades 7 to 12—into junior high schools with grades 7–9 and senior high schools with grades 10–12. Conversion of junior high schools into middle schools began in the 1970s. The motivation behind the development of middle schools and the organization of their curriculum was similar to the basic motivation behind the high school electives movement—the desire to arouse the interests of nonacademically oriented young adolescents in reading, especially adolescents who didn't or wouldn't read much.

The sincerity of the motivation behind the middle school movement cannot be doubted; it was becoming increasingly clear that many non-college-intending students were not motivated by the coursework they took in junior or senior high school and were increasingly unwilling to do homework. What might be viewed as a worrisome portent for the future were rationales for middle schools that were accompanied by sneers at subject matter learning and the general academic orientation of the schools.

A typical comment appeared in a 2001 California Department of Education monograph: "The typically rigid organization of junior high schools, which mimicked the departmentalized structure of secondary education, rendered young adolescents unprepared for the transition from the emotionally safe haven of elementary schools to the demands of the junior high schools."[20] To appreciate this remark, readers need to know that the middle school movement prized an interdisciplinary curriculum in grades 6, 7, and 8—apparently to imitate the "safe haven" of the self-contained elementary classroom.

Whatever the justification, the secondary literature curriculum was permanently altered by a movement that added grade 9 to the high school but split off grades 7 and 8 from the junior high school and put these grades into a school that could include grade 5 as well as grade 6. The academic goals of the junior high school were necessarily weakened in a newly configured school that sought to offer a variety of "exploratory" electives and prioritized the social and emotional needs of young adolescents over academic needs. (For example, courses like grade 8 algebra were considered "barriers" to the full development of a middle school.[21]) However, much greater damage to students' intellectual development may have been inflicted by changes in academic requirements for the prospective teacher in this new educational structure, a topic that has received little attention by researchers interested in teacher quality.

Hidden within the substitution of a middle school for a junior high school was the need for a new kind of teacher (and license) for the span of grades in a middle school. The teacher was called a middle school generalist and was typically prepared as the elementary school teacher was—with minimum requirements for academic coursework. The teacher who had prepared to teach grades 7–12 was not considered appropriately trained for grades 4, 5, and 6 (most teachers who taught either junior or senior high school were apt to be licensed for grades 7–12); nor could that teacher legally teach grades 4, 5, or 6.

As can be seen in a somewhat inaccurate and out-of-date chart on the website of the National Middle School Association showing licensure by state, the grade levels covered by a license for this new educational entity typically span grades 5–8, although a number of states offer this license for grades 4–8 or, worse yet, for grades 4–9.[22] Without this new license, building principals would have considerably reduced flexibility for shifting teachers around to accommodate enrollment bulges and teacher turnover from year to year if students in grades 5 and 6 were in the same building with students in grades 7 and 8.

The middle school movement set in motion a gradual but invisible migration of academically strong teachers. As middle schools became the dominant reality in many states (in Massachusetts, only two junior high schools were left as of the early 2000s), academically strong junior high school teachers tended to move up to the high school level to continue teaching their subject (likely a major part of their motivation to become teachers), according to a high school mathematics department chair during the 1980s.[23] As he noted, most teachers with a strong major in an academic discipline were not interested in teaching fifth or sixth graders, or teaching in self-contained classrooms, teams, or clusters—organizational schemes presumed to reduce the impersonal organization of the junior high school.

Changes were later made in many states to require more academic coursework of prospective middle school teachers after it became clear that a glorified elementary teacher couldn't handle the subject matter of grades 7 and 8, especially in mathematics and science. But middle school teachers today are much less likely to have majored in the subject they teach. As certification information in Massachusetts suggests, the middle school teacher legally licensed to teach any grade from 4–9 frequently turned out to be an elementary teacher who had "added" a middle school license, a licensing regulation in many states often fulfilled by little more than completion of a course in adolescent development.

The major result of the structural "reform" known as the middle school movement was the eventual replacement over time of academically qualified teachers in grades 7 and 8 by academically under-qualified teachers. Given the academically impoverished background of the typical elementary teacher in this country, how could one expect them as middle school teachers to teach a demanding curriculum in any subject in the middle school? Coherent connections to the academic demands of the high school curriculum were thus broken, both by the typical middle school teacher's academic training (or lack thereof) and by the more nonacademic and self-preoccupied nature of the middle school.

CONCLUDING REMARKS

Until well after World War II, English curricula gave high school students a common understanding of the English language and their own civic and literary heritage as English speakers. Moreover, literature curricula were relatively coherent and challenging, even if narrow in aim and content according to "Progressive" educators. The latter had long stressed that the school curriculum should be relevant to students' lives, interests, and perceived needs and above all foster personal growth. They had little interest in discipline-based coursework designed to advance disciplinary knowledge and to prepare students for college.

The electives movement—the breakup of the year-long English course into semester courses that began in the late 1950s—was the first important change in the English curriculum that could be perceived as an effort to implement the philosophy of the early Progressive movement. Designed chiefly to motivate high school students who did not like or seemed not to benefit from the academic orientation of the literature curriculum set in place for all students in the 1890s by the Committee of Ten, the electives movement inevitably undermined its coherence and rigor for most students.

At the same time, the major change in the structure of secondary education undermined the secondary literature curriculum at its roots, elevating social goals over its academic demands. The conversion of junior high schools for grades 7 to 9 to middle schools for grades 4 or 5 to 8 allowed the curriculum in grades 7 and 8 to become the culmination of an elementary school curriculum rather than the introduction to secondary subject matter learning.

English teachers themselves were willing to acknowledge the limitations of a high school curriculum shaped chiefly by electives. But there is as yet no groundswell of concern about the coherence of the middle school literature curriculum (or curricula in other subjects, for that matter) and its relationship to the high school literature curriculum, nor a concerted search for better solutions to the increasing range of interests and skills in young adolescents than either the middle school or the junior high school as an educational institution seems to have provided.

POINTS TO REMEMBER

1. The high school syllabi resulting from work of the Committee of Ten in the 1890s to standardize college admission requirements across the country gave the public high school literature curriculum a coherence and strong academic orientation that lasted over half a century.

2. The surging enrollment of high school students, as well as the increasing range in their reading and writing skills, in the first three decades of the twentieth century led to the development of a variety of academic and vocational alternatives to accommodate them and to a remarkable increase in graduation rates.

3. Most high school students experienced a coherent and challenging literature curriculum, though not an identical curriculum, until well after World War II, when two kinds of structural changes—the break-up of the year-long English course into semester-long elective courses and the conversion of the junior high school into a middle school—reduced its coherence and rigor, especially for the vast middle of the high school student body.

NOTES

1. Peter David Witt, "The Beginning of the Teaching of Vernacular Literature in the Secondary Schools of Massachusetts" (EdD diss., Harvard Graduate School of Education, 1968).

2. Isaac Kandel, *The Dilemma of Democracy* (Cambridge: Harvard University Press, 1934), 26.

3. Jeff Lingwall, "Compulsory Schooling, the Family, and the Foreign Element in the United States, 1880–1900." 2010, http://www.heinz.cmu.edu/faculty-and-research/research/research-details/index.aspx?rid=372.

4. National Center for Education Statistics, *Digest of Education Statistics*, 2008, Table 32. Historical summary of public elementary and secondary school statistics: Selected years, 1869–1870 through 2005–2006. In 1899–1900, there were about 62,000 high school graduates of an estimated 519,000 students enrolled in grades 9–12, with an average of 99 days attended per pupil, ages 5–17.

5. Edward Krug, "Graduates of Secondary Schools in and around 1900: Did Most of Them Go to College?," *The School Review*, 70 (1962): 266–72.

6. http://en.wikipedia.org/wiki/History_of_education_in_the_United_States#Compulsory_laws

7. Claudia Goldin, "America's Graduation from High School: The Evolution and Spread of Secondary Schooling in the Twentieth Century," *Journal of Economic History*, 1998, 58 (2): 345–74.

8. For example, the Marvell School District in eastern Arkansas enrolled 179 students in grades 9–12 in 2009–2010. The Arkansas Department of Education lists 69 different courses being taught; only a handful for individual students. Among Marvell's course offerings are agricultural mechanics, agricultural metals, and agricultural science and technology, as well as AP English language and composition.

9. Kandel, *Dilemma*, 52–53. The existence of small high schools in every state led James B. Conant in his extensive study of American high schools in the mid-1950s to call for a high school with a graduating class of at least one hundred students, asserting that "a small high school cannot by its very nature offer a comprehensive curriculum... Financial considerations restrict the course offerings of the small high schools," *The American High School Today* (New York: McGraw Hill, 1959), 77. Conant advocated a high school of at least 400 students (his ideal was about 750) so that it could provide specialized programs to meet the needs and interests of a broad range of students. He was particularly concerned about the absence of advanced coursework in mathematics and science. While a small high school could offer such programs, Conant believed that the extravagant cost would ultimately be prohibitive.

10. John Valentine, *The College Board and the School Curriculum: A History of the College Board's Influence on the Substance and Standards of American Education, 1900–1980* (New York: College Entrance Examination Board, 1987), 14.

11. George Tanner, "Report of the Committee Appointed by the English Conference to Inquire into the Teaching of English in the High Schools of the Middle West," *School Review,* 1907, 15: 37–45.

12. See, for example, Paul Witty, "Developing Better Reading Skills and Habits in High School Pupils," *NASSP Bulletin,* 1954, 38 (206): 1–6.

13. Leila Christenbury, "The Secondary English Elective Curriculum," *English Journal,* 1979, 68 (6): 50–54.

14. Helen Robinson and Samuel Weintraub, in a 1973 issue of *Library Trends* on reading preferences in grades 6–12, comment that "comparisons of reading interests show that young people, even those who are bright, dislike many of the titles considered to be classics by their English teachers, and even more in recent years than in the past. Moreover, English class is liked least compared to mathematics, science and social studies in all grades from four to twelve."

15. Robert C. Small, Jr., "Framework for Diversity: The Elective English Curriculum," *High School Journal,* 1972, 56 (2): 93–107.

16. Kandel, *Dilemma,* 22–23.

17. Jean E. Brown and Lela B. Phillips, "Maintaining the Human Aspects of English: Electives in the Curriculum," *Language Arts Journal of Michigan,* 1986, 2 (1): 29.

18. James Moffett, *Active Voice* (Portsmouth, NH: Boynton Cook, 1981).

19. For one description of the origins and purposes of middle schools, see http://www.ncsu.edu/meridian/sum2005/middle_schools_on_net/index.html.

20. California Department of Education, "Historical Perspective: Setting the Stage for California's Middle School Reform Movement." *Taking Center Stage,* 2001, 6.

21. http://www.nmsa.org/portals/0/pdf/publications/On_Target/middle_or_high/middle_or_high_2.pdf.

22. http://www.nmsa.org/ProfessionalPreparation/CertificationLicensurebyState/tabid/1235/Default.aspx.

23. Ray Whipple, former chairman of the mathematics department in North Reading High School, Massachusetts, personal communication to author, October, 2000.

4

Abandonment of Intellectual
Goals in the Literature Class

In 1980, the National Council of Teachers of English (NCTE) published a collection of essays titled *Three Language Arts Curriculum Models: Pre-Kindergarten through College*.[1] According to a reviewer, the essays present "three curricular designs broadly representative of current thought and practice: the process or student-centered model, the 'heritage' or traditional model, and the competencies model."[2] Given that the gist of the essays had been guided and approved by the Commission on the English Curriculum, a subcommittee of NCTE, one may safely conclude that these three approaches accurately captured the state of the English curriculum at the time.

What is noteworthy from today's perspective is that in only one of the three models—the heritage model—was literary knowledge viewed as content in the English curriculum, meaning that there were substantive goals for the English curriculum. The heritage model clearly pointed to teacher- or school-selected literary content. On the other hand, the process or student-centered model pointed to a curricular approach that was indifferent to specific literary content; it highlighted "personal growth" supported by student choice of literary content. In contrast to either the heritage or student-centered model, the competencies model sought mastery of skills independent of literary content, whether chosen by the teacher or the student.

The abandonment of familiarity with the literary and civic heritage of English-speaking people as a major goal of the English curriculum and the substitution of non-substantive goals (personal feelings, skills) in its place in the other two models was, in retrospect, the first stage of a process leading to the exclusion within two decades of a coherent and demanding literature curriculum as the intellectual heart of the entire English curriculum. This chapter shows how literary study began its journey from center stage in the English class to the wings—to serve there as an occasional handmaiden to personal expression and as the basis for attitude formation, a distinctly nonliterary goal.

NEW SOURCES OF INCOHERENCE

The incorporation of writing process approaches stressing experience-based writing into the elementary curriculum in the 1970s (often called a workshop approach) and their spread soon afterwards into the middle school curriculum meant almost a free choice of titles (by student or teacher) as the literature curriculum, at least from grade 7 to grade 10. Coherence might be found in a historical approach to American literature and British literature in grades 11 and 12 if year-long survey courses on literary movements in these bodies of literature were still offered.

But suddenly there was a new kid on the block. From the 1970s on, what was called multicultural literature became the rage. The problem was its attitudinal thrust, not the inclusion of new works into the literature curriculum—a process that had always taken place, albeit slowly.

The movement to include if not forefront multicultural texts ultimately negated whatever possibility remained for re-establishing coherent sequences of literary works whether at one grade level or across secondary grade levels but with more contemporary titles presumed to appeal to adolescent readers than were on the old College Board-required list. Mounting criticism of the electives movement had led many high schools to restore year-long courses at some grades, but with some electives still available, particularly in the senior year.

When it burst upon the educational scene in the early 1970s, multiculturalism seemed to be a philosophy about curricular content. It claimed to be ethnically inclusive, concerned with civic goals, and motivated by good will in its efforts to address perceived omissions in the curriculum. Elizabeth Fitzgerald Howard, a writer of children's books, suggested that if the "purpose of literature is to liberate, the purpose of authentic multi-cultural literature is to help liberate us from all the preconceived stereo-typical hang-ups that imprison us within narrow boundaries."[3]

No reasonable person quarreled with the notion that some high quality literature by or about members of different social groups in this country should be included in the secondary English curriculum (although many experienced English teachers were critical of incorporating contemporary texts that required little instruction because they were already "accessible" to students on their own). Nor did reasonable people disagree that American children should be able to see the multiethnic nature of the country they inhabited, as well as a broad range of peoples around the world, in the literature they were asked to read in the elementary school.

The broad literary goals trumpeted by the first wave of multicultural educators were positive ones, for young students especially, whether or not there would ever be evidence that the inclusion of multicultural works enhanced the self-esteem or academic achievement of "non-mainstream" students. And they remain desirable goals, despite the continuing low academic achievement of black and Hispanic students and the absence of research to suggest that multicultural texts motivate young students to do more reading of any kind on their own.

When multicultural literature entered the literature curriculum as such, its chief but not sole focus was, understandably, works by black writers about black Americans. The void that needed to be addressed was obvious in the major literary anthologies for English teachers in the 1960s.

One high school English teacher, Mary Hawley Sasse, noted that a widely used high school literature anthology, *Adventures in American Literature,* "devoted just ten of its 827 pages to nonwhite writers of the United States."[4] These ten pages included "three spirituals and a poem by black Americans; and a lament, a song, and a two-page 'story' by Native Americans." Another anthology, *The United States in Literature,*[5] "included even fewer selections: three spirituals and two poems by black American writers."[6]

The author's color was not consistently the explicit feature separating ethnic from nonethnic literature in the early 1960s. That is because *ethnic* could be used at the time to designate an immigrant group from any continent in the world, in addition to blacks and the indigenous inhabitants of this country. The meaning of *ethnic,* however, swiftly changed from an identifiable linguistic or religious group to an artificial racial category—from a term that could apply to hundreds of groups in this country to a term much, much narrower in application.

Interestingly, the title of Sasse's essay was and still is absolutely correct in its description of this country. America is a multiethnic culture. But from the beginning, the term *multiethnic* was always confused with *multicultural,* as if most of America's ethnic groups could be considered distinct cultures in this country in any meaningful sense of the word. The imprecise thinking that lay behind the constant interchange of all these terms was symptomatic of the ever-evolving crusading spirit of the times.

In the late 1960s, curriculum planners eager to redress the neglect of black writers in particular began to expand the literature available to students, most often as part of separate elective courses at the high school level called "minority literature" or "American ethnic literature." Sometimes these courses included works about European ethnic groups.

Inclusion of works about European ethnic groups was clearly the case in anthologies of ethnic literature offered by both educational and non-educational publishers. While works by black writers were almost always featured in these compilations, they also tended to include literature about Irish Americans, Jewish Americans, and Italian Americans. This kind of inclusiveness is quite visible in the ethnic-oriented anthologies that appeared in the late 1960s and early 1970s, such as *The Outnumbered,*[7] *Speaking for Ourselves,*[8] *Minorities All,*[9] and *A Gathering of Ghetto Writers: Irish, Italian, Jewish, Black, and Puerto Rican.*[10]

The point here is simply to demonstrate that ethnicity was not coterminous with race at the time, that the ethnic experience (except for blacks and those referred to as Native Americans) was understood as an immigrant experience, that the immigrant experience quite visibly included the experiences of European ethnic groups, and that the ethnic or immigrant experience was seen as a transitional experience as newcomers became acculturated as Americans. When the shift from the term "minority" to "multicultural" began in the 1970s, however, it coincided with the notion that the ethnic or immigrant experience should not be seen as, and should not be, a transition into the American mainstream.

By the mid-1990s, the immigrant experience of European ethnic groups—indeed, their very existence—was no longer acknowledged in elementary school reading series as well as high school literature anthologies.[11] Multicultural literature was now much narrower in scope and a clear reflection of academic politics, especially in education schools. Its goals could no longer be described as academic or as broadening.

Anthony Appiah, a philosopher sympathetic to the impulse behind the initial conceptualization of multiculturalism, criticized what he called "illiberal multiculturalism" in 1997 in an essay in the *New York Review of Books*. He charged it with seeking to "close young people off into identities already ascribed to them" and to enable them to evade personal responsibility for their thinking or behavior because—according to illiberal multiculturalism—both were determined by their "culture" or "race, ethnicity, or gender."[12]

By the mid-1990s, "diversity" consisted of a small set of categories, with only an occasional example hinting at the real ethnic diversity of this country. For example, in 1995 Scott Foresman put out an anthology called *Multicultural Voices* that it recommended as an elective supplement to its literature anthology series for grades 7 to 12.[13] Although the four-page yellow brochure describing the supplement stated that the anthology "celebrates the immense diversity of American culture" and includes recent works by "Americans of varied cultural backgrounds—African, Asian, Hispanic, Native American, European, and Middle Eastern," this description was highly misleading. Almost all the works were by members of the four affirmative action categories, and there was exactly one work about an identifiable European ethnic group: "The Wooing of Ariadne" by Harry Mark Petrakis. This story stood out like a sore thumb in this collection.

On the other hand, an anthology entitled *Multicultural Perspectives*, published by McDougal, Littell in 1993 as part of its *Responding to Literature* series, made a clean sweep of European ethnic groups—a sort of literary ethnic cleansing, if you will. Apparently its editors and consultants had decided that only members of the four affirmative action categories had retained their "cultural identities" and had "unique heritages" that could enrich America.[14]

Literary ethnic cleansing had profound consequences for the content of high school literature programs. A seemingly benign movement dedicated to the inclusion of quality literature by authors or about groups almost invisible in the traditional curriculum had invisibly morphed into a movement leading to the selection of texts that had little literary quality or were not literary in nature at all, such as family chronicles, ordinary diaries, or outright advocacy journalism.

Multiculturalism came to conceptualize diversity in very narrow terms not only within this country but outside its boundaries as well. Publishers of three leading literature anthologies in the 1990s provided brochures to inform state departments of education, school districts, and teachers exactly what selections and authors contributed to their multicultural offerings.[15] The authors and groups highlighted in descriptions of their "multicultural" content were restricted for the most part to those in our four affirmative action categories and to the ethnic kin of African, Asian, and Hispanic Americans in their countries of origin. The extraordinary range of ethnic and religious diversity among people of European descent was barely acknowledged if at all in the selections in these three major anthology series.

A few smaller publishers sometimes exhibited more imagination in the categories they called multicultural possibly because they were confused by—or resistant to—the evolution from ethnicity to the spurious racial framework constructed from the four affirmative action categories. As one example, in its 1994 pre-K–6 catalog, the publisher Sundance included along with "cultures" reflecting the four major affirmative action categories four "vanishing cultures:" the Australian Tiwi, Finnish Sami, Sherpas and Tibetans, and Nomadic Tuaregs.

The battle over who was in and who was out was not over by the end of the 1990s despite the seeming monopoly by "cultures" presumed to represent the four affirmative action categories on the ethnic content in our readers and literature anthologies. A prominent bone of contention among those promoting multicultural literature was whether groups judged to be "of color" should be the chief or only ethnic groups featured in multicultural curriculum materials.

Should the label *multicultural* be reserved for groups "most excluded and marginalized," as one educator put it? Although she cited no empirical evidence to support this statement, Violet Harris, an education professor at the University of Illinois, wanted the focus on "people of color" because they "tend to be the most excluded from literary canons, recommended booklists, and elementary curricula."[16] Hawaiian educator Kathryn Au repeated Harris's assertion that literature about the groups in the four affirmative action categories generally lies outside the literary canon, recommended book lists, and the elementary school curriculum.[17]

It is highly unlikely that this could have been a valid description of any recommended booklist or curriculum by the 1990s. However, evidence to back up their assertions was never the strongpoint of self-described multicultural educators.

While Harris's perspective suggested that other groups might have been eligible for inclusion as multicultural (they just weren't that marginalized or excluded), not so, apparently, for Rudine Sims Bishop, a professor of education at Ohio State University.[18] Bishop was emphatic that multicultural literature was about "people of color" and only about "people of color," whether in this country or elsewhere. Not only did color determine diversity, Bishop claimed, she also believed that "people of color" have cultural values, attitudes, and behaviors that differ from those who are white and middle class. She did not specify what these values, attitudes, and behaviors were.

Unhappy with the set of artificial racial categories recommended in Harris's, Au's, and Bishop's textbooks for teachers (as well as in many others), Eileen Iscoff Oliver, an education professor at Washington State University, implied that a potentially limitless number of groups could sail under the flag of multicultural literature.[19] In yet another NCTE publication, Oliver sought to challenge "Eurocentric" values by promoting not only literature by members of the four affirmative action categories, but also Jewish literature and literature on physical and mental disabilities, Vietnam veterans, older adults, the homeless, homosexuality, and teenage suicide. Explicitly arguing for a broad definition of *multicultural*, she suggested that it could designate any group that has the characteristics of "otherness."

Oliver was joined in battle by members of the American Library Association (ALA), also seeking a more inclusive notion of multicultural literature. Hazel Rochman, assistant editor at *Booklist*, a review journal of the ALA, was adamant about the definition she offered in 1993.[20] To Rochman, "multiculturalism means across cultures, against borders," and "doesn't mean only people of color." In a professional show of support for her position, her book won an award in 1994 for the best professional book by and for librarians published in the previous three years.

Expansion of the groups eligible for inclusion on library shelves for multicultural literature had already taken an interesting turn in a 1992 book edited by Carla D. Hayden, director of the Enoch Pratt Free Library in Baltimore, Maryland.[21] The groups her book covered were: African American, Arabic, Asian, Hispanic, Jewish, Native American, and Persian, a bizarre mélange from any perspective. Elevation of the Persians as one of this country's seven major cultural groups was simply yet another indication of the complete incoherence of the multicultural literature movement by the 1990s.

However benignly multicultural literature came into the curriculum in the 1960s as a way to teach students about this country's ethnic diversity, it had rapidly evolved into a set of chiefly non-ethnic, politically-defined categories. These categories could be extended to an endless number of other groups, depending on the discovery of new social causes and the academic, professional, social, or political credentials of their advocates.

Even though affirmative action categories were from the outset inaccurate social science categories, it clearly didn't matter. Expansion of the literary/nonliterary content of school reading programs in the name of multiculturalism was animated by arbitrary notions of what was *not* "Eurocentric," in large part a moralistic stance against the old College Board-required titles and their early replacements from British or American literature.

As the multicultural movement merged with "critical pedagogy" (to be discussed in a later chapter), it came to involve "questions about power, status, and the political and economic functions of literature as well as its aesthetic functions."[22] As a result, the choice of selections for a secondary literature program often reflected little attention if not deliberate inattention to the literary quality of a work (e.g., the choice of *Malcolm X* instead of a work by Richard Wright or James Baldwin).

Equally problematic, choice tended to reflect little attention to the text's level of reading difficulty for an English class in a high school. As English teachers incorporated into their classroom curricula nonliterary as well as literary selections to promote the attitudinal goals of multiculturalism, they, in effect, reduced the time their students spent studying literary texts of high quality and at an appropriately challenging level of reading difficulty.

By the 1990s, a majority of high school students were experiencing an incoherent and distorted literature curriculum. Their curriculum had first been reduced in difficulty and rendered intellectually incoherent in the 1960s and 1970s by electives, middle school interdisciplinary curricula, and reading/writing workshop approaches. It had then been reshaped in the 1980s by a moralizing pedagogy that had incorporated texts useful to its attitudinal goals and succeeded in banishing many of those that weren't, especially if they were difficult and had to be taught first.

Students who took traditional American and British literature survey courses and Advanced Placement literature or language classes did not experience an undemanding literature curriculum. But they could not avoid the manipulative moralizing that had already begun to affect these courses as well.

PROFESSIONAL SOURCES OF INTIMIDATION

Prospective English teachers absorbed a moralizing pedagogy from their preparation programs, often in the name of compensatory or social justice (more on this in Chapter Seven). Those already in the teaching force absorbed it from their professional development programs. A third and equally powerful source accelerated the influence of this moralizing pedagogy: English teachers' own professional journals and the guidelines and curricular materials put out by major publishers. With reason, publishers catered to what professional leaders, prominent education school faculty, education researchers, and curriculum specialists told them was needed in the literature curriculum in order to sell their wares. The coordinated influence on ambitious new English teachers who sought to become professionally active, and their effects on possible resisters, cannot be overestimated.

In teachers' professional literature, withering sarcasm drove out reasonable professional arguments about demanding works that had long been in the curriculum for historical and cultural reasons. Clever invectives were applauded by the academy as well as by professional leaders themselves. And their users were readily and regularly given publication space.

As one example, we look at the comments of three English educators in four reviews of the leading literature anthologies published in 1989.[23] All four reviews were published between 1989 and 1991 in the *English Journal*, the leading journal for English teachers in this country. In them the three reviewers consistently expressed an animus against works written by "dead writers" or, as they were called in one review, "DOWGs" ("dead old white guys"). Literary selections written by DOWGs, they declared, "will not inspire students to learn nor teachers to teach and learn." In their view, students "must be empowered to make and respect their own decisions about what they read."

The reviewers' self-contradictory assumptions were clear. Students should be able to choose what they want to read so long as the works are not by dead writers. Works by dead authors have nothing to say to contemporary adolescents, especially if the dead writer was a white male. So much for empowering students. Instead of making a case for the works of those living writers the reviewers believed deserved to be anthologized, they chose mostly to attack the dead. They complained that "nearly half of the poets among the recent literature selections in a grade 11 anthology were dead" and saw this "homage to the dead" continuing in its grade 12 anthology.

The reviewers even scorned the recent dead who in some cases spoke from "alternative literary traditions" themselves, despite being "white." For example, the reviewers described Harry Mark Petrakis (a Greek-American writer) and Bernard Malamud (a Jewish-American writer) as the most "geriatric" short-story writers in a grade 11 anthology. On the other hand, in the same review, they praised the inclusion of a "deeply moving letter by Bartolomeo Vanzetti on the eve of his execution." That Vanzetti was also a dead white male did not matter in this case.

Not only did most authors become irrelevant upon death, they also automatically entered the ranks of "conservatism." A poetry section in one anthology was scorned for its "conservative list of authors" precisely because it contained few "living" authors. In all four reviews, the word *conservative* was regularly applied as an epithet to any anthology or any section thereof with too many dead writers to suit the reviewers' taste. Anthologies for grades 11 and 12, the only two years of literary study that must include the past if they address the history of American and British literature, were almost consistently criticized for not including enough of the present, even though the present was amply provided for in other years.

Altogether, sarcastic and unprofessional reviews or articles made clear that the quality of the literary works in teachers' closets or literature anthologies was of little interest. The color, gender, and vital signs of the authors were, apparently, the critical features to watch for.

The sarcasm expressed in the professional literature for English teachers was cleaned up by educational publishers for their publication guidelines, but their own brand of moralizing turned out to be more ridiculous than unprofessional. A prime example of the illiberal version of multiculturalism is the set of guidelines for "reflecting diversity" put out for "educational publishing professionals" by Macmillan/McGraw-Hill in 1993.[24]

Macmillan/McGraw-Hill's Credo, appearing in the introduction to the guidelines, asserted that it was committed to presenting students with "an unbiased view of the full range of human potential." The document explained that the "great strides" that have been made "toward acknowledging diversity" in recent years have occurred only because "countless people have spoken out against social prejudice." But despite these "great strides," editors must maintain eternal vigilance and "guard against social bias and ethnocentrism."

To avoid muddying the picture of who was the object of bias, Macmillan/McGraw Hill indicated that it had decided to exclude all European groups in this country on the grounds that it would focus only on groups "that have been historically omitted from educational materials" (even though most European ethnic groups had also been historically omitted). To allay any concerns that it might whitewash the behavior of European Americans, Macmillan/McGraw Hill asserted it would not "deny the conditions under which persons of color have lived, or sidestep the issue of European American participation in creating these conditions," such as "slavery" or "migrant- and factory-labor exploitation."

In some cases, Macmillan/McGraw Hill would apparently present certain figures just to spite European Americans. It declared its textbooks would be careful not to confine themselves to the "most widely accepted African-American poets or writers" or show a preference for African American political figures that are "acceptable to the European-American establishment." Macmillan/McGraw Hill didn't indicate what it would do if African American political figures acceptable to the "European-American establishment" were also acceptable to African Americans.

Finally, Macmillan/McGraw Hill suggested that careful warnings should be given in teacher guides about the sex-role and ethnic-group stereotypes lurking in our literary classics if classic tales are included in literature anthologies. Here crept in the notion that perhaps these anthologies would be better off without this apparently tainted material. It was clear that editors and their consultants should be highly suspicious of literary classics before including them.

The specter of self-censorship looms large here. Would an English teacher dare to choose a literary or nonliterary text about turn of the twentieth century sweatshops that exploited Italians, Irish, and Jewish workers, or the exploitation of Irish as well as Chinese workers in the building of transcontinental railroads, or the use of Italian labor in building the New York City subway? Not if she was aware that the details contradicted the notion that exploitation is a sin committed only by white people against nonwhite people. Macmillan/McGraw Hill's injunctions were not unique to this company; it was simply one of the first major publishers to lay out its catechism in black and white.

What was touted as a movement to broaden students' horizons ended up narrowing and distorting them. As Richard Bernstein commented in an insightful analysis of the evolution of multiculturalism in our national culture, "it is a universe of ambitious good intentions that has veered off the high road of respect for difference and plunged into a foggy chasm of dogmatic assertions, wishful thinking, and pseudoscientific pronouncements about race and sex."[25]

CONCLUDING REMARKS

The addition of literary texts highlighting the ethnic diversity of this country could have taken place as part of an evolution of our secondary literature curriculum from chiefly classical works in the nineteenth century, to mainly British literature at the turn of the twentieth century, and to more American works by the late twentieth century. It might have naturally included a few contemporary American texts, as well as older and newer European, Latin American, and other works.

Instead, the multicultural advocates and presentists (those judging the past with contemporary moral perspectives) sought to banish by denigration the literary texts or authors in the curriculum that hearkened back in spirit if not in actual title to what was on the original College Board-required lists. Denigration of older literary works in the English language as "canonical," "Eurocentric" or "American-centric" was increasingly accompanied by calls, however indirect, for the exclusion of these works from the curriculum on the grounds that their audiences, if not their authors, were "oppressors" of those whose works were replacing the older titles (but at too slow a pace to satisfy the denigrators).

What was not pointed out was that older works, British or American, were typically much more difficult works to read than their replacements in the literature curriculum. Experienced high school English teachers could easily tell the difference. But the stark differences in reading difficulty (or the lowering of the difficulty level of the literature curriculum by the particular multicultural texts that were chosen to replace older works) never appeared as a topic of discussion or research in their professional literature.

Once the goals of the multicultural movement became almost wholly attitudinal, that is, they had no sincere cognitive thrust (i.e., to expand cultural and historical knowledge), one may wonder about the effects on the broad middle of our students. There had to be a downside in assigning literary texts in the English class to achieve noncognitive goals, even if the topic was never publicly discussed.

Carol Jago, a longtime English teacher at Santa Monica High school, noted that so many "second-rate texts were being used for literary study... that literary study seemed pointless...for these simplistic, one-dimensional, largely autobiographical novels."[26] The waste of instructional time on texts not worthy of literary study deprived students of instructional time on texts that could contribute to intellectual growth. But who could say this in a school or at a professional conference?

POINTS TO REMEMBER

1. By 1980, the English curriculum could be described by three models. In only one of the three was literary knowledge an intellectual goal. Competencies or choice dominated the other two.

2. Multicultural literature was introduced as such in the early 1970s and at first promised to broaden students' cultural horizons and thinking. By the late 1980s, its goals were no longer cognitive but attitudinal.

3. The secondary literature curriculum was incoherent and less undemanding as easier or mediocre multicultural texts replaced more demanding works in the curriculum on ever-changing political grounds.

NOTES

1. Barrett Mandel, ed., *Three Language Arts Curriculum Models: Pre-Kindergarten through College* (Urbana, IL: National Council of Teachers of English, 1980).

2. Faye Louise Grindstaff, "Review of *Three Language Arts Curriculum Models: Pre-Kindergarten through College*," *College Composition and Communication*, 1983, 34 (2): 225–27.

3. Elizabeth F. Howard, "Authentic Multicultural Literature for Children: An Author's Perspective," in *The Multicolored Mirror: Cultural Substance in Literature for Children and Young Adults,* ed. M. Lindgren (Fort Atkinson, WI: Highsmith Press, 1991), 91–92.

4. Published by Harcourt, Brace and World, 1963.

5. Published by Scott Foresman, 1963.

6. Mary Hawley Sasse, "Literature in a Multiethnic Culture," in *Literature in the Classroom: Readers, Texts, and Contexts*, ed. Ben Nelms (Urbana, Il: National Council of Teachers of English, 1988), 168.

7. Edited by Charlotte Brook, Dell, 1967.

8. Edited by Lillian Faderman and Barbara Bradshaw, Scott Foresman, 1969.

9. Edited by Gerald Leinwand, Washington Square Press, 1971.

10. Edited by Wayne Miller, New York University Press, 1972.

11. See Sandra Stotsky, *Losing our Language* (New York: Encounter Books, 2002), Chapter 3.

12. Anthony Appiah, "The Multicultural Misunderstanding," *New York Review of Books*, October 9, 1997, 30–34.

13. *Multicultural Voices: Literature from the United States* (Glenview, IL: Scott Foresman, 1995).

14. David Foote, Margaret Grauff Forst, Mary Hynes-Berry, Julie West Johnson, Basia C. Miller, and Brenda Pierce Perkins, *Multicultural Perspectives* (Evanston, Il: McDougal, Littell, 1993), 4.

15. "Multicultural Experiences" is the title of the brochure accompanying Holt, Rinehart and Winston's *Elements of Literature*, 1992; "Multicultural Authors and Selections" is the title of the brochure accompanying McDougal, Littell's *Language and Literature*, grades 9–12, 1994; and "Multicultural Representation in Literature and Fine Art" is the title of the brochure accompanying Prentice Hall's *Literature*, 1994.

16. Violet Harris, ed., *Teaching Multicultural Literature in Grades K–8* (Norwood, MA: Christopher-Gordon Publishers, 1993), xvi.

17. Kathryn Au, *Literacy Instruction in Multicultural Settings* (Fort Worth, TX: Harcourt Brace Jovanovich, 1993).

18. Rudine Sims Bishop, *Kaleidoscope: A Multicultural Booklist for Grades K–8* (Urbana, IL: National Council of Teachers of English, 1994).

19. Eileen Iscoff Oliver, *Crossing the Mainstream: Multicultural Perspectives in Teaching Literature* (Urbana, IL: National Council of Teachers of English, 1994).

20. Hazel Rochman, *Against Borders: Promoting Books for a Multicultural World,* ALA Books/Booklist Publications (Chicago: American Library Association, 1993).

21. Carla D. Hayden, ed., *Ventures into Cultures: A Resource Book of Multicultural Materials and Programs* (Chicago: American Library Association, 1992).

22. Violet Harris, Review of *Against Borders: Promoting Books for a Multicultural World* by Hazel Rochman, *Journal of Reading Behavior*, 1994, 26 (1), 119.

23. Bruce Appleby, Greg Johnson, and Robert M. Taylor, "A Hefty New Literature Series: Something for Everything?" *English Journal*, 1989, 78 (6): 77–80; "Another Hefty Literature Series: Cutting the Costs." *English Journal*, 1990, 79 (4): 92–96; "An Old Standard: Scott, Foresman's *America Reads* Series." *English Journal*, 1990, 79 (6): 86–90; and "Yet Another Standard: HBJ's *Adventure* Series." *English Journal*, 1991, 80 (7): 93–96.

24. *Reflecting Diversity: Multicultural Guidelines for Educational Publishing Professionals* (NY: Macmillan/McGraw Hill, 1993).

25. Richard Bernstein, *Dictatorship of Virtue: Multiculturalism and the Battle for America's Future* (NY: Alfred Knopf, 1994).

26. Carol Jago, e-mail message to author, January 5, 1998.

5

How NCTE Encouraged Deeper Literary Chaos

By the end of the twentieth century, the major organization for high school English teachers had ensured that a coherent literature curriculum could not be reconstructed as part of a secondary English curriculum. It had prevented this possibility with the national standards it set forth in 1996 and with its negative position on recommended reading lists of any kind. In this chapter, we look at the status of literary study embedded in the 1996 standards and the strategies used to prevent development of a recommended reading list to accompany them.

THE 1996 NCTE/IRA STANDARDS

In 1996 the National Council of Teachers of English (NCTE) and the International Reading Association (IRA) jointly released national standards for the English language arts and reading. Use of the word *standards* is deceptive because no independent reviewers ever considered the twelve statements posing as standards in the document as standards—substantive objectives or guidelines for what students should know as well as be able to do in a specific discipline. It was clear at the outset that no coherent sequence of literary works in the English curriculum could be constructed from them. The document did not offer a clear standard to guide language learning, either.

When the NCTE/IRA document containing these twelve so-called standards was made available to the public in 1996, after *five* years of work funded in large part by taxpayers, the document was broadly criticized by a *New York Times* editorial as well as by significant public voices. A senior adviser to the Secretary of Education in the Clinton administration was quoted as saying: "It looks more like a statement of philosophy that provides some background and grounding for professionals in the field." The then president of the American Federation of Teachers candidly declared: "They are not standards at all....They also throw out the best hope for getting some kind of equity among our widely disparate English curriculums."[1]

The 1996 document has never been revised. It remains the official professional view of objectives or guidelines for the K–12 English language arts curriculum and provides little ground to justify the widespread hostility (if not outright opposition) among NCTE members, especially high school English teachers, to both sets of Common Core's standards for them, its college and career readiness standards and its grade-level standards.

In addition to what was already taking place in the English classroom, how did the 1996 document further contribute to the shrinking of literary study? To begin with, it addressed literary study in only two of its twelve standards.

1. Students read a wide range of print and non-print texts to build an understanding of texts, of themselves, and of the cultures of the United States and the world; to acquire new information; to respond to the needs and demands of society and the workplace, and for personal fulfillment. Among these texts are fiction and nonfiction, classic and contemporary works.
2. Students read a wide range of literature from many periods in many genres to build an understanding of the many dimensions (e.g., philosophical, ethical, aesthetic) of human experience.

To better appreciate this grudging admission that the study of literature was still part of the English curriculum, one should remember that the secondary English curriculum had been conceptualized for over one hundred years—since English became a major subject in the high school curriculum—in three major strands: literature, language, and composition.

By mentioning literary study in only two of twelve standards, the NCTE/ IRA document implied that it was, or should be, a small part of the total English curriculum.

Literary study was to share classroom time, so the document conveyed, with activities needed to meet such other so-called standards as "Students develop an understanding of and respect for diversity in language use, patterns, and dialects across cultures, ethnic groups, geographic regions, and social roles." This latter standard would likely lead to more moralizing by the teacher than intellectual growth or English language learning by students. Only graduate students and professors in linguistics or anthropology would be equipped by training to explore "diversity in language use, patterns, and dialects across cultures, ethnic groups, geographic regions, and social roles" in an academically meaningful way.

The NCTE/IRA document also demoted literary study by the way in which it classified literary texts. They were simply one of many different kinds of "text." To be sure, the document took care to point out that "texts that we call 'literary' have a special function in our culture and in student learning." But the very first standard made it clear that literary texts would have to compete in the English class with a "wide range of print and non-print texts" if students are "to build an understanding of texts, of themselves, and of the cultures of the United States and the world."

One should not underestimate the variety of "print texts" alone that students were to study, according to the NCTE/IRA document. They ranged from novels and poems to popular journals, letters, family and "community" documents, and the writing of their peers, which the document expressly urged in order to "build self-confidence" and mutual "respect."

In addition to this vast compendium of "print texts," students' reading experiences were to include an equally vast range of what the NCTE/IRA document called "visual texts." This peculiar concept, which implied that "print texts" are not texts that can be seen, was intended to designate such things as illustrations, television, advertisements, multimedia resources, and an infinite host of other kinds of "graphic and visual messages."

The NCTE/IRA document also provided classroom examples that suggested how to reduce even more the little time that students might have for studying authentic literary works. These examples implied, among other things, that students ought to spend the bulk of their time in literary study discussing the history and culture of the country from which the literary work comes and relating it to their personal lives or contemporary issues, especially when the racial identity of students in an affirmative action category was involved.

The variety of efforts by the NCTE/IRA document to drastically shrink the time for authentic literary study in the curriculum and to distort its essence was driven explicitly by nonacademic ends. Although the document admitted that literary works are "valuable not just as informative or communicative vehicles, but as artistic creations and representations of human culture at particular times and in particular places," it nevertheless proposed that works for classroom study should be chosen for "relevance to students' interests" and their "roles in society and the workplace." It did not suggest consideration of literary quality or cultural significance.

As the document made clear in its discussion of its first standard, the purpose of students' experiences with "text" was to enable them "to view and critique American and world history and contemporary social life." In other words, the study of a literary work was to serve as a springboard for class discussions on a vast range of social studies topics, not to develop literary taste or literary knowledge.

How to Turn the English Class into an Ersatz Social Studies Class

The exploitation of literary study for political purposes—one goal of multicultural educators—can be seen in the following excerpts from a December 1997 article in the *English Journal,* the major journal for English teachers. It was written by a high school English teacher to show how she used class time when addressing contemporary literature.

> Students need to read accessible, worthwhile, relevant, controversial, and contemporary literature....Thus, I teach Raymond (sic) Rodriguez's *Hunger of Memory*, Toni Morrison's *Beloved*, Michael Dorris' *A Yellow Raft in Blue Water*, and Tim O'Brien's *In the Lake of the Woods*. One serendiptity (sic) is that my students can use "school to work" skills by writing letters to authors (the dead make poor correspondents).
>
> ...The material in the three novels and one autobiography is potentially explosive. After my students and I discuss, briefly, the issues involved— racism and prejudice are common threads in all four—I have the students read the first chapter....

...much work is required regarding history, geography, societal values, and psychology. I send my students out to cull the Internet, history books, magazines, and movies for information and misinformation regarding the themes and ideas in these works—affirmative action, slavery, Native Americans, and Vietnam. Class days are spent in cooperative learning groups disseminating the material gathered....

The unit [on Vietnam] begins with a two-day video on the background of Vietnam up to the Gulf of Tonkien (sic) resolution. The county's social studies coordinator then visits my classes and shows slides of his tour of duty in Vietnam. Students also need to learn some geography at this point and the U.S. presidents involved (Eisenhower through Nixon).

The next day I take a bowl filled with marbles—ratio of white marbles to black ones being 10:1—reflecting the approximate ratio of the two races in the United States in 1965. I proceed to remove white marbles (which represent caucasians) and enumerate reasons: college deferment, professional jobs, National Guard. We then read the poem, Vietnam #4, and discuss its premise that blacks were deliberately used as cannon fodder during the Vietnam War.

In cooperative reading groups the students read different articles concerning war crimes: the massacre at My Lai, the Nurenberg (sic) trials, and Lt. William Calley. Using the jigsaw technique, they change groups and share their information. A Socratic seminar the next day focuses on the question: "Should one obey immoral laws?" This will later form the nucleus of discussions on Martin Luther King, Jr., the Holocaust, and the Japanese internment.[2]

As indicated, this English teacher chose four contemporary books for "literary study" because they were "accessible," "worthwhile," "relevant," and "controversial." What she meant by "accessible" is not clear (easy to read?), but her belief that all four books were united, to a greater or lesser extent, by a focus on racism and prejudice suggested what she thought was worthwhile, relevant, and controversial.

Social and political criteria did more than determine the choice of literary works for her students to read in the English class *and* the topical connections she encouraged them to see among these works. These criteria also motivated and justified the use of other kinds of materials. As indicated, she spent two days of class time showing students a video on Vietnam ("up to the Gulf of Tonkien resolution") and then arranged to have them spend yet another day viewing the slides an ex-veteran took of his tour of duty in Vietnam.

This English teacher's students spent many hours gathering information on such topics as affirmative action, slavery, Native Americans, and Vietnam, and discussing this material in class in "cooperative learning groups." While studying Tim O'Brien's novel, they spent even more hours listening to their teacher's views on why there were more blacks, proportionately, than whites in our armed forces in Vietnam and then discussing the charge that blacks were deliberately used as cannon fodder during the Vietnam War (a charge, or topic, not addressed in the novel).

Students also spent time reading about and discussing such events as the My Lai massacre, the Japanese internment, the Holocaust, and the Nuremberg Trials, and holding a "Socratic seminar" on "Should one obey immoral laws?" Most of these topics are not related to the Vietnam War and were not addressed in these four literary works.

Nevertheless, this English teacher apparently saw all these topics stimulated by Tim O'Brien's novel. Worse yet, she also felt that she could bring academic authority to classroom discussions of these topics, even though one might assume that her disciplinary training was in English, not history. Her students clearly spent much of their time "learning" from each other while they discussed social studies topics, "learning" from her lectures on social studies topics, "learning" from audio-visual materials on social studies topics, and "learning" from her social studies colleague. What is not clear is whether they spent much time learning from the literary works she assigned with respect to what their authors had actually written, despite the title of the article.

How to Turn the English Class into a Creative Arts Class

The examples in the NCTE/IRA document also encouraged teachers to stimulate "creative" (and often non-verbal) responses to a literary text (such as "storyboards"), with the further hint that such classroom projects might substitute for a "traditional essay." Many examples of such "creative" responses can be found in the December 1997 *English Journal* article excerpted above. When the class studied Michael Dorris's book, students (1) drew "pictures" for several pages of relevant quotations the teacher had taken from the book, (2) listed "names they had been called" (especially "racial slurs") and wrote a "vignette concerning one of the names," and (3) engaged in a "creative response" as a culminating activity to Dorris's work such as a "collage," selecting "songs for some of the main characters," or writing a "Jeopardy game" or a "children's book."

Even if the creation of the NCTE/IRA document had not cost about three million dollars, one would be justified in raising questions about its antidisciplinary stance and political pretensions. One might also wonder how the two organizations responsible for guiding the construction of literature programs and the teaching of literature in our schools were able to get thousands of English teachers across the country (who were given some of these millions for meeting and discussing various drafts of the standards document) to support it, if in fact they did.

Influence on State Standards

The effort to downgrade the status and content of literary study in the NCTE/IRA document extended to many state standards documents for the English language arts written in the 1990s. NCTE and IRA members were active in the development of their own state's English language arts and reading standards, and the staff at a department of education would naturally look for guidance to the major professional organizations for English and reading teachers.

In an op-ed essay appearing in a 1997 Los Angeles newspaper, Carol Jago, a teacher at Santa Monica High School and the director of the California Reading and Literature Project at the University of California at Los Angeles, noted that many "curriculum standards documents being written overlook the study of literature as an important and lasting outcome of a high-school education."[3] She judged this a "serious omission" and then went on to provide six reasons why students should study literature.

What must give one pause here is not so much what Jago wrote in this op-ed essay, but the fact that she felt the need to write it at all. Who would have thought, even fifteen years ago, that an English teacher would feel compelled to write an op-ed essay *arguing for* the study of literature in high school?

In Jago's opinion, the state standards writers who were recommending the study of informational texts, films, and multimedia resources in place of literature in secondary school English classes were being influenced by the "cry of employers for graduates with workplace literacy." However, it is doubtful that employers or the business community were the chief influences on standards writers. It is more likely that the leadership of the major professional organizations responsible for guiding the work of English language arts educators, as well as the academic influences on them, was a stronger influence on standards writers.

But Jago's observations about the lack of attention to literature in state standards documents were right on target. They were confirmed by the results of a 1997 survey of twenty-eight state standards documents for the English language arts by the Thomas B. Fordham Institute,[4] by a 1998 research report on state standards in the English language arts by the Council for Basic Education (CBE),[5] and by a 2005 review of all state standards documents for the English language arts by the Thomas B. Fordham Institute.[6]

Literary study did not fare well in most of the twenty-eight documents examined in the 1997 survey. In some state documents (e.g., those for Missouri, Tennessee, and Minnesota), objectives for literary study were mixed indiscriminately with objectives for reading and were minimal in number as well as excessively general in content. The authors of the 1998 CBE report also noted that many state English language arts standards "do not address literature study (e.g., reading literature of particular time periods and genres)."

It is difficult to believe that most high school English teachers were indifferent to the study of literature, given that it is probably the passion for literature that inspired them to become English majors and then English teachers. Had high school English teachers who cared about literary study been excluded from writing committees charged with developing state standards? Had staff at state departments of education listened only to English and reading education faculty in their state's schools of education? Had writing committees consulted only the leadership of the two organizations that had spent five years and several million dollars to come up with twelve mostly content- and culture-free statements to guide the content of the K–12 English and reading curriculum? We don't know.

Despite the concerns expressed in the 1997 Fordham review and the 1998 CBE report, those in charge of revising state English language arts standards in the next decade clearly paid no attention. The 2005 Fordham review of all fifty states' standards documents noted that most states provided no general standards outlining the content of the literature curriculum, never mind in an intellectually coherent way. The study of American literature by name was not required in about half of the states, and the two-word phrase was barely mentioned in many others. Only a few offered examples of titles, authors, literary periods, and literary traditions as indices of reading level or literary quality or as milestones in the history of the English language.

A literary standard requiring the reading of texts representing "the diversity of American cultural heritage and cultures of the world" (Wisconsin) or "universal themes, diverse cultures and perspectives, and the common aspects of human existence" (New Jersey) does not bespeak broad-mindedness. Rather, it points to an unwillingness to make professional judgments about what pre-college students should actually study or learn.

Nebulous standards could and did maintain the ever-changing curricular smorgasbord for literary study already experienced by students, with little or no coherence across a state's school systems and classrooms to promote intellectual growth. With a literature curriculum shaped by culture-free and content-light standards, students could continue to graduate with (1) no understanding of the themes, characters, images, and sources of inspiration that define the body of literary works called American literature; (2) no knowledge of the classical and British roots of American literature and their continuing influence on today's writers; (3) no insight into the influence of American writers on this country's political, religious, economic, intellectual, and social history; and (4) a limited grasp of this country's public language—the language of its civic life and seminal civic documents.

However, the fact that a dozen states had provided some content-rich and content-specific literature standards, sometimes accompanied by recommended reading lists, demonstrated that it was possible, even with a strong tradition of local control, to outline the substantive content of the secondary literature curriculum in an acceptable way. That Common Core's English language arts standards did not provide such an outline in 2010 serves as a reminder of the sources of influence undermining the coherence of the secondary literature curriculum for half a century.

Sources of Influence on the NCTE/IRA Standards

The first source is clearly the English teachers' own professional organization. But NCTE itself is strongly influenced from above and below. The high school English teachers who may still comprise the bulk of NCTE's individual membership, and for whom the organization was founded in 1911, are directly influenced about what texts to teach and how to teach them in their coursework in undergraduate English departments and education schools.

In addition, as for teachers of other high school subjects, the academic goals of English teachers are seriously undermined by the academic limitations of elementary and many middle school teachers, and the emphasis of their professional organizations on skills, processes, and strategies, not the demands of discipline-based content. Their professional organizations cannot admit, for professional reasons, that discipline-based knowledge is the basis for acquiring "deep conceptual understanding" or for being able to think like a member of the discipline.

As NCTE must have found out through its partnership with the IRA in developing national "standards" in the 1990s, K–8 reading teachers are not trained to teach poetry, drama, fiction, and nonfiction. (Nor, it must be said, are English teachers trained to teach reading.) Reading teachers are typically *not* English majors, who have (or should have) a deep understanding of American and British literary texts, literary traditions, and literary movements as the basic credential for teaching secondary English.

In addition to diagnosing weaknesses in basic reading skills, reading teachers are trained to teach content-free reading strategies, processes, and skills—to all students. Their academic background and professional training leave them underqualified and unprepared to conceptualize a sound framework, and implement a sound foundation, for a coherent secondary literature curriculum. Unfortunately, K–8 reading teachers now belong in large numbers to NCTE as well as to IRA, the organization founded for their interests, indicating the influence from within on the NCTE/IRA standards, as well as non-literary from the partnership with IRA.

OPPOSITION TO LITERARY GUIDELINES

The continuing existence of the 1996 NCTE/IRA standards remains a prime example of the disciplinary and moral confusion in the organization to which legislators and other citizens would normally turn for guidance in their effort to re-establish, or in some cases to construct for the first time, a coherent and demanding literature curriculum for all students. Today as in the 1890s, such a curriculum must be constructed not just for those students whose homes are limited in the resources they can provide but also for the increasing number of students with home languages other than English. This widespread confusion shows up most clearly in what was considered the greatest shortcoming of the 1996 document—the absence of a recommended list of authors, works, literary periods, or literary movements at each educational level.

The bankruptcy of its intellectual framework for literary learning can be seen in the utter vacuity of the one "content" standard that it offers on literary knowledge. Standard Two proposes that "students read a wide range of literature from many periods in many genres to build an understanding of the many dimensions (e.g., philosophical, ethical, aesthetic) of human experience."

In a half-hearted attempt at greater specificity, the document suggests that literary reading should encompass both "classic and contemporary" works— a polarizing and invalid distinction. To illustrate this nonliterary distinction, the document offers S. L. Hinton's *The Outsiders*, a piece of adolescent literature written in 1967, as one example of a "classic literary text."

The failure of the 1996 NCTE/IRA document to provide a conceptual framework for literary study was a severe disappointment to many educators and other citizens. Indeed, one major reason why the U.S. Department of Education chose to discontinue its funding of the NCTE/IRA standards development project in 1994 was the absence of any effort to address this central topic in the interim draft submitted by the two organizations.[7]

However, a deeply felt professional need for NCTE to create a recommended list of authors, works, or literary movements existed at the heart of NCTE itself, although the heated debate over a recommended reading list that took place was never reported on by the media. During his tenure as president-elect and then as a president of NCTE in 1997–1998, Sheridan Blau, professor of English and education at the University of California in Santa Barbara, made a strenuous effort to gather together NCTE members interested in creating such a list and to develop an authorized list that "might supplement the NCTE/IRA standards document."[8] He was aided by Carol Jago, then chair of the NCTE Commission on Literature, who later became a president of NCTE, in 2009–2010.

Blau forthrightly declared that NCTE had a professional responsibility to provide a recommended list to English language arts teachers and to the public.[9] In 1997 and 1998, he scheduled meetings at every major NCTE conference of what was called the National Literature Project.

Unfortunately, very little was done at these meetings because the NCTE members who did not want any list developed attended these meetings and took up most of the time scheduled for the meetings arguing their position and preventing those who did want to create a list from even discussing their ideas. In other words, those who opposed the creation of a list engaged in a filibuster against their own colleagues. What few people outside NCTE and the academic world in which the debate originated understand to this day is why the opposition to the creation of any list at all was so fierce and how it affected the development of Common Core's secondary English language arts standards in 2010.

In proposing these meetings in 1996 and 1997, Blau gave three reasons why he and others thought "it might be in our professional interest to produce professionally authoritative reading lists to guide curriculum planners, school boards, parents, teachers, and students who ask if there is anything like an authorized reading list to guide them in planning reading programs." He first placed the creation of an authorized list in the context of professional control. As he pointed out, "such lists—and they are fairly narrow ones...exist in the common practices and book-room inventories of schools nationally and in the contents of textbooks. It's time that we took control of professional decisions that we have heretofore yielded to the power of tradition and the market research of textbook publishers."

Blau then pointed to the need for a common culture. "In a nation as diverse as ours," Blau remarked," we must count on schools to provide the materials for building a common culture beyond that created by commercial TV and popular music." He added that a "nationally honored program of reading can help to shape such a culture to compete with and deepen the culture now produced by the media."

Blau's third reason concerned the educational value for teachers of simply discussing the construction of a national list. "The debate over what selections or authors to include on any national list," he explained, "will itself be a useful for teachers and their students to engage in and may prove more intellectually valuable than any lists thereby produced."

How did the opponents of a list respond to these reasons? The e-mail messages sent by NCTE members to each other on a dedicated interactive website for the topic give a good flavor for the range of arguments against the creation of a national reading list. Some members waved the banner of local control. Some bemoaned the energy consumed by discussions of what to include. Yet others expressed the traditional antiauthority stance of many English teachers.

As one writer put it, "the lists could easily become prescriptive." "Approved lists," this writer noted, "have a way of becoming sacred...and then we become embroiled in arguments about what should be included and excluded." Another writer thought an authorized list "would turn disastrous in the hands of too many misguided administrators." Yet another agreed that textbook publishers "dictate our reading habits and choices" but supported an ever-evolving annotated reading list compiled by teachers and maintained by NCTE.

Many letters against an official list on these grounds were published in the April and September 1998 issues of *The Council Chronicle*. Blau had alluded to the hypocrisy of this position in a July 1998 issue noting that the Council had adopted at its Executive Committee meeting in April 1998 a reading list under the title of "Guidelines for a Gender-Balanced Curriculum in English, Grades 7–12."

In its essence, however, the dispute was not about which works or authors should be on a recommended core list, even though a great deal of heat has always been generated when English teachers attempt to construct such a list as part of an official curriculum development committee at the local or state level. The dispute was about core questions that have not been articulated to parents and others supporting the public schools.

Does this country still have a common civic culture and a common language to use for participation in that culture? If so, do English teachers have a professional obligation to acknowledge and maintain them? If not, should there be many different kinds of public schools to reflect the other "cultures" the critics claimed to see, each with their own curriculum? Many opponents of a recommended reading list didn't think we had a common culture, didn't want one, or wanted to change whatever it is, but didn't address the major implications of their oppositional stance.

One high school teacher expressed clearly in his e-mail the bedrock judgment about the existence or desirability of a common culture. "Trying to push and generate common culture in America is useless and misguided," he asserted. "It will never happen and shouldn't happen." One opponent of a common culture questioned Blau's motives. A college instructor, she wondered if the "purpose of a school is to provide the materials for building a common culture," but she was more concerned about how "culture and power work" and the "complex motivations of those wanting to have a National Reading List." She saw a National Literature Project promoting (unnamed) "vested interests."

Other opponents thought this country's institutions needed to be changed, although they didn't say what should happen to the public schools. "Canonlists," another college instructor asserted, "are features of a past era...They keep diversity in check...they slow change and are... benchmarks against which to measure literacy...We're in an age of transition and cultural transformation...Lists are tools for maintaining a stable version of literacy...Institutions that attempt to maintain stability in the face of change are in conflict with the times. They are at best nostalgic, at worst, barbaric." Quoting from a book titled *Tradition and Revolution*, he wrote: "the real menace of barbarism is that it tends to be hidden behind a facade of respectability, in institutions which are so taken for granted that the very idea of subjecting them to criticism is received as an intolerable heresy."

It's hard to identify what Western country this writer is referring to. The only countries where criticism of existing political institutions is an "intolerable heresy" are the dictatorships in non-Western countries.

An earlier president of NCTE participating in this e-mail conversation did make it very clear who some of the "real" barbarians are. "To my mind," she wrote, "creating a literature canon is counter to all we have stood for and worked for through the years. And, if you [the current president] will pardon the insult, I think this sounds like something Bennett or Hirsch would propose...Our efforts would be far more well-placed if we worked on helping teachers, administrators, and school districts learn how to select quality literature for their particular populations. A canon will be a handicap, not a help."

The view that "particular populations" needed their own literature curriculum has been endemic among NCTE leaders. This belief is why so many academicians and educators in NCTE have relentlessly excoriated E. D. Hirsch Jr. for his advocacy of "cultural literacy" in 1987 and steadfastly ignored the curriculum materials produced by his Core Knowledge Foundation.[10]

Anyone defending a list as necessary for a common culture was immediately attacked, as the following example shows. Two high school teachers, after expressing their desire to see a competent reading list in their school district because "anything has got to be better than the pathetic contents of the bookroom now," strongly affirmed that we "have a common American culture—not a Euro/Anglo one." They went on to exclaim that they want a "canon" which "reflects all those lofty ideals of freedom, individualism, enterprise, and ingenuity (for better or for worse) which color every aspect of our history, from the Boston Tea Party to Ellis Island."

One of their critics saw these lofty ideals as nothing more than a matter of class interests and an expression of hypocrisy. She claimed that a "common culture exists in the minds of middle class whites." "The problem with selecting a canon that reflects 'all those lofty ideals' is that those lofty ideals historically have only applied to certain segments of the population ...If we are so concerned about those lofty ideals, why do so many of us insist that all students read the same book at the same time? And why do we pick the book? Doesn't democracy belong in a classroom that teaches about the lofty ideals of democracy?"

Another critic sought to deny that there are distinctively American values or a common culture: "those ideals don't sound like Native American values (except for freedom, which was denied to them by those who came supposedly embracing that ideal) so I think those ideals sound very Anglo/European...This country has never had one unifying culture, despite attempts to make us all melting pot pink. The strength of this country is in its diversity. *Vive La Difference*."

SUPPORT FOR LITERARY GUIDELINES

At the very time the battle over a recommended reading list was taking place at the national level out of public view, the same battle was taking place in Massachusetts but with a very different outcome. In contrast to those successfully filibustering NCTE members at meetings designed to discuss a recommended national list, English teachers in the Bay State favored a recommended list, it turned out.

In 1996–1997, a new committee appointed by the Bay State's commissioner of education and the chairman of its board of education was charged with revising a draft of K–12 English language arts standards. This draft had been originally developed in 1995 by a different group of English educators and unanimously rejected by the former board of education and chairman. One of the charges to the committee was to develop a recommended reading list.

After much internal bickering, the committee fulfilled the charge with an interesting compromise: two recommended lists of authors (not titles) sorted by broad educational levels, known as Appendix A and Appendix B. Appendix A consisted of dead black and white authors whose writings were considered to constitute the civic and literary heritage of English-speaking people; Appendix B consisted of contemporary authors, in the United States or elsewhere. Authors for grades K–8 in both appendices had been vetted by the editors of *The Horn Book*, the leading children's literature quarterly in the country and well known to many Massachusetts teachers.

All Massachusetts teachers were sent copies of these draft appendices (along with the revised draft standards) for public comment and asked to evaluate them on a five-point scale ranging from disapproval to high agreement. The individual evaluations sent back to the state's department of education were overwhelmingly positive; in response to a specific question about the two suggested lists of authors, two-thirds "agreed" or "agreed strongly" with their contents and approved inclusion in a standards document.[11] The final document therefore recommended that school and classroom literature programs draw from both lists.

The broad support these two lists received throughout Massachusetts in 1997 showed that when given an opportunity to express their views without intimidation or harassment, most English language arts teachers believe they share a common literary culture and wish to preserve it. In fact, the lists have been drawn on by different groups of English teachers from year to year when selecting reading passages for the state's annual assessments in English language arts, a fact that can be verified by a perusal of the grade-level test items released annually and posted on the Department's website, a legislative requirement.

As Sheridan Blau later observed, most of the writers opposing the creation of a national reading list were college-level instructors, not high school

English teachers. High school English teachers may still comprise the majority of NCTE members, but they do not comprise a clear majority of voting members on its Executive Committee or Board of Directors.[12] English teachers favoring guidelines for a secondary literature curriculum have been consistently misled, scorned, and certainly outwritten in academic or professional journals. But when given an opportunity to let their views be known, without harassment, ridicule, or shunning, they do. They know better than anyone else the limitations of the incoherent curricula they teach.

As a validating postscript, a committee of Massachusetts English teachers was convened in the fall of 2010 to recommend additions to the Common Core English Language Arts Standards that had been adopted by the Massachusetts Board of Elementary and Secondary Education in July 2010. They unanimously recommended the addition of Appendix A and Appendix B to the final (and current) document.

Earlier, these two appendices had been rejected for addition to Common Core's own standards document (by representatives of other state departments of education and probably others) on the grounds that most states did not want recommended lists of authors or titles,[13] a long-term victory by those who had successfully prevented any recommended title or author list from accompanying NCTE/IRA's 1996 standards and their own state standards.

An illuminating example of what one newspaper-reading "community" actually thought were the "top ten books every informed citizen should read" also came out of Massachusetts in 1997. The following titles, here ranked in the order of frequency of mention, were sent in by readers of *The Boston Globe* in March 1997 in response to a solicitation by the newspaper: (1) the *Bible*, (2) *The Adventures of Huckleberry Finn*, (3) *Hamlet*, (4) *The U.S. Constitution*, (5) *Moby-Dick*, (6) *The Declaration of Independence*, (7) *The Odyssey*, (8) *The Federalist Papers*, (9) *Crime and Punishment*, and (10) *A Tale of Two Cities*.[14] *The Globe*'s (very literate) readership is not considered "conservative" or uninformed.

Another illuminating point needs to be made about this *Globe* list. Although most Americans might think that three of the titles in this list—*The U.S. Constitution*, *The Declaration of Independence*, and *The Federalist Papers*—are beyond argument (i.e., that no one could argue against the presence of these specific texts on a suggested national reading list), this is not the case.

At NCTE's national convention in 1995, an English educator participating in a small group discussion of a draft of the NCTE/IRA standards declared outright that the inclusion of *The Declaration of Independence* on any suggested reading list was a "canon" question.[15] That is, she saw no reason why all students should be compelled to read it since it reflected the thinking of those dreaded and dead white males. That kind of thinking was part of the context and "grassroots" discussions from which NCTE/IRA's final standards emerged.

The social and political goal of many of the English educators who successfully opposed the creation of a suggested national reading list was to eliminate students' respect for this country's civic culture. They sought to discredit it because they believed it was irredeemably tainted by the original sin of racism and by what they perceived as its enduring oppression of nonwhite males and females of all colors. To discredit this country's civic culture and transform it into one they believed would bring about social justice as they defined it, they encouraged a moralizing pedagogy in the English class, as exemplified by the article in the *English Journal*.

However, the century-long emphasis on authentic literary study as the central purpose of the English class has been a major obstacle for their moralizing fervor. Culturally and critically esteemed works of literature do not lend themselves easily to remedying social injustice; their themes and characters are usually complex, and they take time to teach. Moreover, those works traditionally taught at the high school level tend to contain advanced vocabularies and many literary allusions and historical references, and thus require more advanced reading skills and literary knowledge than the middle grades have ever demanded.

CONCLUDING REMARKS

The changes in the secondary literature curriculum that occurred in the 1980s and 1990s went hand in hand with a conscious policy by NCTE leadership to demote the status of literary study in the English curriculum. It did so in two ways. First, by means of the standards it issued in 1996, which mention literary texts in only two of its twelve standards and imply a reduction in the amount of time devoted to the study of authentic literature. Second, by its opposition to a recommended reading list, thus disallowing in advance the possibility that a work perceived as "canonical" would appear on one.

In addition, many other educators, beyond those in public schools or English education, helped to turn many high school English classes into mock social studies classes. The political issues that had come to dominate secondary literary study by the 1990s had long consumed colleges and universities. Questions of race, class, and gender had already become the main perspectives through which to examine literary works at the post-secondary level.

By the mid-1990s literature had been stripped of its status as a "privileged discourse" in college and university English departments, and the object of study was now "textuality," which could be studied in anything labeled a text, ranging from comic books and campaign posters to popular song lyrics.[16] The professional journals and organizations used by higher education faculty, the courses taught in English, humanities, composition, or education departments, the textbooks they advised on, and the research or scholarship they did all contributed to the diminished role of literary study in the high school curriculum and to the incoherence of its literature curriculum.

NCTE's failure to highlight the role of literature in the English curriculum in its 1996 standards can be seen as a reflection of a cultural and political shift that had already taken place in leading college and university English departments—as well as a reflection of its association with the IRA. But in encouraging teachers through its conference sessions, official journals, and other publications to use cultural or historical material to "contextualize" the literary works they did assign, NCTE's leadership and English education faculty were subverting the educational process itself.

English teachers could not, on the basis of their academic coursework or professional training, judge its accuracy and adequacy. But no historians, political scientists, or sociologists were vetting contextualizing material chosen often extemporaneously by a classroom teacher. Instead of critical thinking, which many leading educators claimed they were developing (and still do), NCTE was in effect supporting emotion-laden, misinformed, and incoherent thinking.

POINTS TO REMEMBER

1. The leadership of English teachers' major professional organization diminished the role of literary study in the secondary curriculum by means of the standards they created with the IRA in 1996 and by their opposition

to any kind of recommended reading list, leaving schools without the resources to guide the construction or reconstruction of a coherent literature curriculum.

2. The standards NCTE created in 1996 in partnership with the IRA strongly reflected the influence of skills-oriented reading teachers and the political perspectives of higher education faculty. This standards document then influenced the development or revision of many state standards documents, leaving them both impoverished and politicized.

3. The 1996 NCTE/IRA standards document is still the official document of NCTE and provides no guidelines for constructing a coherent literature curriculum that could address the content-empty and culture-free College and Career Readiness Standards developed by the Common Core initiative.

NOTES

1. These and other critical comments, including those in a *New York Times* editorial, are all cited with references in Henry Maloney, "The Little Standards That Couldn't," *English Journal*, 1997, 86 (1): 86–90.

2. Elfie Israel, "What Contemporary Authors Can Teach Us," *English Journal*, 1997, 86 (8): 21–23.

3. Carol Jago, "Study of Literature Can Work Miracles with Teens," *The Outlook*, Friday, December 12, 1997.

4. Sandra Stotsky, *State English Standards: An Appraisal of English Language Arts/Reading Standards in 28 States* (Washington, DC: Thomas B. Fordham Foundation, 1997).

5. Scott Joftus and Ilene Berman, *Great Expectations? Defining and Assessing Rigor in State Standards for Mathematics and English Language Arts* (Washington, DC: Council for Basic Education, 1998).

6. Sandra Stotsky, *The State of State English Standards, 2004* (Washington, DC: Thomas B. Fordham Foundation, 2005).

7. In a news release from NCTE headquarters in Illinois on May 11, 1994, President Janie Hydrick is quoted as noting "several philosophical differences" between NCTE/IRA and the U.S. Office of Educational Research and Improvement, which had just announced in March that the grant for continuing the development of the standards project would not be renewed. According to Hydrick in the news release, the standards project had been "criticized for failing to address the 'issues' of 'a particular canon' for children's literature." Her response: "an expanding body of children's literature [is] part of our evolving understanding of developing literacy."

8. Sheridan Blau, "Should We Create a Professionally Authorized National Literary Canon?" Announcement on NCTE Talk, the NCTE List Serve, 1996–97.

9. Sheridan Blau, Presidential Column, *The Council Chronicle*, July 1998.

10. See, for example, Walter Feinberg's review "Educational Manifestos and the New Fundamentalism" of *The Schools We Need and Why We Don't Have Them*, by E. D. Hirsch, Jr., *Educational Researcher*, 1997, 26 (8): 27–35.

11. Source: Massachusetts Department of Elementary and Secondary Education.

12. Sheridan Blau, e-mail messages to author, November 21, 1997, and December 28, 2011.

13. Jeff Nellhaus, Director of Assessment for Partnership for Assessment of Readiness for College and Careers (PARCC), personal communication to author, October 20, 2010.

14. On March 3, 1997, in a brief article entitled "What Should We Read?," *The Boston Globe* invited "readers to write or e-mail us their own Top 10 lists of most important books, and we will publish a Readers List of those most frequently named."

15. Personal observation.

16. Sheridan Blau, personal communication to author, December 28, 2011.

6

How an Incoherent Literature Curriculum Slows Down Intellectual Growth

Publication of FORUM 4 in Fall 2010 led to a highly spirited discussion of the findings of the national survey by a group of high school English teachers from this country and Canada on English Companion Ning.[1] They agreed that the literature curriculum in this country is incoherent. The high placement rates in "developmental" reading courses for freshmen at two-year and four-year public colleges, as well as the growth of college-sponsored summer/fall freshman reading programs, reflect to a large extent the major deficiencies in the high school literature curriculum.

How could incoherent high school literature programs have slowed down intellectual growth sufficiently to leave a large number of students simply unready for credit-bearing college-level work at the age of eighteen, or ready only for a book with a low reading level? We look first at coherence in a collection of short stories that is familiar to most high school English teachers to understand its cognitive implications before addressing the question.

WHAT COHERENCE LOOKS LIKE IN A LITERARY READER

James Moffett and Kenneth McElheny's *Points of View* (1966 original edition, 1995 revised edition) is a collection of over forty short stories from different literary traditions and historical periods (the revised edition does not have the international scope that is so prominent in the original edition). *Points of View* shows different ways in which the fictional techniques used to tell a story—the narrator's stance—can be classified.[2] The stories are exemplars of many different kinds of points of view, but that alone doesn't establish the coherence of the collection.

Coherence is established by the classification and ordering of the stories. They have been classified and ordered along a dimension of learning that may move, depending on what is being classified, from easier to more difficult, personal to impersonal, concrete to abstract, subjective to objective, simple to complex, or from the past to the present. However this dimension moves, it does not necessarily imply a higher qualitative status for its endpoint. For example, *Crime and Punishment* may be psychologically more complex than *Charlotte's Web,* but one would not praise the former as a better work of literature because of that. The way in which the short stories in *Points of View* are classified and ordered enables students to gain insights they could not acquire from a random ordering of these literary narratives.

Moffett proposed a progression of literary points of view that moves from the completely subjective or personal to the completely objective or impersonal. The sequence begins with interior monologue, dramatic monologue, letter narration, diary narration, subjective narration, detached autobiography, and observer narration and ends with anonymous narration (single character point of view), anonymous narration (dual character point of view), anonymous narration (multiple character point of view), and anonymous narration (no character point of view).

Moffett's *Active Voice*, officially published in 1981 but circulated in unpublished form many years earlier, outlined a series of writing workshops ordered along the same dimension used in *Points of View*. The series also moved from the subjective to the objective and entailed changing relationships among the audience, the subject, and the writer with respect to distance.

A sequence of narratives that reflects movement along a cognitive dimension facilitates more than a broader understanding of the different stances from which a story can be told. At one level, after reading a number of short stories throughout *Points of View*, students have presumably learned that there are many variations in the point of view from which a story can be narrated, each with its own demands on the author, effects on the reader, and relationship to the story's meaning. That knowledge alone will enrich their reading and understanding of other narratives.

But the particular sequence in *Points of View* does more than enable students to deepen their understanding of the controlling element of a work of fiction. It helps them to appreciate in the final point of view (anonymous narration or no character point of view) the psychological complexity and literary skill required in presenting an objective point of view. The insights gained from a coherent progression of topics, texts, concepts, or activities in a particular discipline can give students the basis for a deeper level of analytical thinking and learning in that discipline.

A coherent curriculum in any subject in K–12 identifies content-based and content-related concepts within a grade and across grades and sequences them in a way that results in cumulative learning if not deeper insights in that subject. Students end up knowing more than they could have learned from randomly sequenced topics, concepts, texts, or activities because they have been given an integrating direction for them. There is an intellectual goal. Without intellectual goals, there is incoherence. And once the curriculum is incoherent, reading levels are affected.

EFFECTS OF INCOHERENCE ON READING LEVELS

As part of their preparation to become certified, many teachers were told that the opportunity to read a book of one's choice, or certain kinds of books (with characters that looked like them) would motivate students to read and to read more than they otherwise would. (And this may have occasionally happened.) So their curricula focused on skills, processes, and strategies, not on texts with important ideas, characters, plots, or striking uses of language with more difficult vocabulary. In this case choice trumped the very meaning of a curriculum.

Inattention to the lack of increasing difficulty in secondary school literary texts was also (and still is) justified by many English education faculty or researchers on the grounds that there is no such a thing as a reading level for a book. However, experienced English teachers know that there is a difference between a text's reading level and its literary features and thematic maturity. Teachers in the Arkansas focus groups, for example, did not hesitate to judge (correctly) the reading level of the literary texts they had to use in the Smart Step Literacy Lab program or in America's Choice's literacy intervention program (fifth grade level).[3]

It is a matter of common sense that the difficulty level of what students read should by definition, increase regularly from grade to grade if they are to be able to read mature adult texts in every subject by the time they reach grades 11 and 12. It is not possible to use primary sources in a grade 11 course on the Constitutional Period if the vocabulary and syntax in students' history textbooks through the grades consistently resemble the vocabulary and syntax in a *Curious George* picture book!

For several generations many high school English departments have organized their literature curriculum with little explicit attention to stretching students' reading capacity far beyond the reading levels of the texts they choose or that their teachers have chosen for them. Yes, many of the books teachers choose to assign at the high school level (e.g., *Of Mice and Men, The Color Purple, The Grapes of Wrath*) have adult themes and are, qualitatively, complex texts. But if most texts consist chiefly of the informal talk of contemporary daily life, then students are not being prepared to read noncontemporary literature (e.g., Frederick Douglass's autobiographies), this country's founding documents, or most contemporary or older adult fiction or nonfiction. The incoherence of the secondary literature curriculum has inevitably meant a decline in the reading level of what students study (and a deceleration of their intellectual growth) in ways that can be documented.

Easy-to-Read Contemporary Literary Texts in High School

The easiest way to prove this point is to compare the readability levels of titles that reflect diversity with those that continue to be denounced by English educators as pointing to the existence of a "Eurocentric or Anglocentric curriculum" (as in Allison Skerrett's article on the high school literature curriculum in a 2009 issue of NCTE's research journal).[4] Here are readability levels for once-popular titles mentioned so few times by teachers in the 2010 national survey that one may assume they are on their way out of the literature curriculum: *Great Expectations*, RL 9.2; *The Merchant of Venice*, RL 9.4; *Silas Marner*, RL 9.7; *A Tale of Two Cities*, RL 9.7; *Hamlet*, RL 10.5; and *Oliver Twist*, RL 11.3. Keep in mind that, except for *Hamlet*, these titles tended to be taught in grades 9 and 10 not so long ago.

As another example from personal experience, New England high schools years ago routinely paired in grade 9 *The Merchant of Venice* with *Ivanhoe*, RL 12.9. The contrast in how their authors portray a central character (Shylock and Isaac of York respectively) in this within-course sequence was educational. Both works are now gone from the curriculum.

In contrast, here are readability levels for some newer titles that may have replaced some "Eurocentric or Anglo-centric" titles in the name of cultural diversity: *The Kite Runner*, RL 5.2; *The House on Mango Street*, RL 4.5; *Giovanni's Room*, RL 5.9; *The Joy Luck Club*, RL 5.7; *The Way to Rainy Mountain*, RL 5.9; *Things Fall Apart*, RL 6.2; *Their Eyes Were Watching God*, RL 5.6; *The Secret Life of Bees*, RL 5.7; *Fallen Angels*, RL 4.2; *Bless Me, Ultima*, RL 5.4; and *The Color Purple*, RL 4.0. All were mentioned a few times in the national survey.

It should be noted that many novels with high readability levels (such as *Ivanhoe*, RL 12.9) were long ago replaced by "Anglo-centric" novels with much lower readability levels, as suggested by the curriculum in the suburban Massachusetts school Skerrett examined. For example, Level 2 students (Level 1 is the most challenging) read in grade 10 *Old Man and the Sea* (RL 5.1) and *Of Mice and Men* (RL 4.5) and in Grade 11 *The Catcher in the Rye* (RL 4.7) as well as works with much higher readability levels. Other examples can easily be found in Renaissance Learning's 2011 report of what students across the country most frequently read: in grades 9–12, *The Outsiders* (RL 4.7) is fourteenth in frequency of mention, and *Speak* (RL 4.5) is sixteenth.

These observations are in no way intended as an argument against choosing titles for cultural diversity or as a slighting of the literary quality or thematic complexity of the books with low readability levels mentioned above. The point is that schools do not seem to have replaced books with demanding vocabulary and complex sentences once in the grade 9 or 10 literature curriculum for the middle third of our students (e.g., *Great Expectations*) with exemplars of cultural diversity whose readability levels are above the elementary level.

It isn't clear, moreover, why non-"Eurocentric" works whose readability levels are at the seventh and eighth grade level were not more frequently mentioned in the 2010 survey, given the clear push for diversity over the past three decades. Here are some examples of such titles and the number of times they were mentioned in the national survey, if at all: *Black Boy*, RL 7.4 (mentioned only four times in the 2010 study); *Invisible Man*, RL 7.2 (mentioned twice); *Namesake*, RL 7.2 (mentioned once); and *House of the Spirits, Love in the Time of Cholera*, and *One Hundred Years of Solitude*, RL 8.4, 9.2, and 8.7 respectively in their English translations (none mentioned at all).

Skerrett's study makes clear that the readability level of a non-"Eurocentric" book is considerably lower, and its length shorter, than the book it replaced. She noted: "in describing efforts to provide a more responsive and motivating curriculum to students who were labeled as low achieving," the department head in the suburban school conflated "multicultural literature with young adult literature, both outside the canon of Eurocentric literature," and "perceived these texts as lacking in academic rigor and even sometimes containing profane content that was inappropriate for school."

Skerrett further quoted the department head as saying: "A dilemma is trying to find books that are more accessible to our students in terms of the interests and in some cases...level of language...because...kids don't read that much anymore. So to get them to read these novels with these very complex sentences, it's tough. So we have had this conversation about expanding the offerings to more multicultural books or shorter books of high interest." Even if Skerrett is unwilling to acknowledge the intellectual differences among these texts with respect to textual features, the English teachers she reported on can see them (some works have more "complex sentences" than others).

Aside from the possible influence of their own undergraduate education, there is one good reason why suburban English teachers in Skerrett's study continued to teach a "Eurocentric or Anglo-centric" curriculum. They were appropriately teaching high school students to read high-school-level books, and they should have been commended instead of castigated. A few works with advanced vocabulary and complex sentences (*The Scarlet Letter, Pride and Prejudice,* and *Frankenstein*) do appear in the top forty titles in Accelerated Reader's database for grades 9–12 (see Table 2.1 in Chapter Two). Invariably, they are among the works denigrated as "Eurocentric" or "canonical."

On the one hand, Skerrett charges these teachers with teaching "sacred educational knowledge" only to able readers and depriving low-achieving students of access to the status of "the ruling classes." On the other, she criticizes them for not catering sufficiently to the undefined perspective of unnamed diverse groups in the school—a condescending attitude to these students at best. Skerrett can't have it both ways.

It may be more beneficial to teach some "sacred educational knowledge" to all students in this school, and to teach more of this knowledge to those who read faster than others (which the school does by means of its leveled courses), rather than to assign short and easy books that ill prepare all students for more demanding reading if not higher education itself. Skerrett's ambivalence (if not self-contradiction) points to educational issues that should be openly addressed in public forums that include students' parents rather than decided upon by educators or researchers in their own narrow professional circles.

The easy multicultural and young adolescent titles now in vogue in the curriculum for almost all students also ill prepare them for the quality of the literary nonfiction that Common Core's standards require English teachers to assign. Such historical and scientific nonfiction as David McCullough's *1776*, RL 9.1; Dava Sobel's *Longitude: The True Story of a Lone Genius Who Solved the Greatest Scientific Problem of His Time*, RL 9.7; Mark Kurlansky's *Salt: A World History*, RL 9.7; and Gordon Wood's *The Americanization of Benjamin Franklin*, RL 10.9 are extremely well-written narratives, but these works will be accessible only to students who experience a curriculum that prepares them to read some high-school-level literature with high-school-level readability scores.

Elementary-Level Literary Texts in the Middle School

Needless to say, the reading problem doesn't begin in grade 9. It is centered in the middle school (grades 6–8), especially for the broad middle third of our students. One clear example of the problem is a middle school curriculum disguised as a professional development program, dubbed the "Arkansas" method, that consists of a classroom library of trade books from which students choose, with guidance from their teachers, as many as twenty-five books for their year's reading.[5] In such a classroom, twenty-five different books may be read simultaneously and thus only common skills can be taught.

Equally problematic, Smart Step Literacy Lab's recommended list of titles (*So Many Books, So Little Time*) consists almost wholly of young adult literature written yesterday: for example, *The Juvie Three*, 2008 (RL: 4.9); *Revenge of the Cheerleaders*, 2007 (RL: 5.0); *Skeleton Creek*, 2009 (RL: 4.8); *The Dreadful Revenge of Ernest Gallen*, 2008 (RL: 4.1; and *Death by Bikini*, 2008 (RL: 4.4). Arkansas English teachers said the program was spreading like kudzu up into the state's high school classes as well as into other states, and that students were not prepared for the titles many grade 9 teachers preferred to teach.

Arkansas teachers also noted that America's Choice, the "turnaround" partner for many low-performing Arkansas schools in recent years, imposed on most students in the high schools its consultants visited a regimen of books "at the fifth or sixth grade level," as well as specific pedagogical strategies. Only students "protected" in an Advanced Placement class by a College Board-approved syllabus, the teachers noted, were exempt from America's Choice's ideas about what high school students should read.

The middle or junior high school is still viewed as the weakest link in the K–12 chain. While most middle or junior high schools across the country do not use the particular programs described above, the literature curriculum in grades 7 and 8 is unlikely to prepare students for the academic demands of a strong high school literature curriculum.

This was not the case in the 1940s, to judge by the most popular titles in a survey of fifty thousand students in grades 7–12 in New York State by George Norvell, state supervisor of English at the time. The most popular titles in grades 7 to 9 included *Kidnapped, Captains Courageous, Treasure Island,* and other books with readability levels at the seventh, eighth, or ninth grade reading level, most of which were probably in the junior high school literature curriculum.

CAN COMMON CORE HELP?

While Common Core's literature standards cannot help English teachers develop a coherent literature curriculum, they aim to increase reading levels in the secondary grades in two ways. First, Common Core provides two content standards in grades 11/12:

> Demonstrate knowledge of eighteenth-, nineteenth- and early-twentieth-century foundational works of American literature, including how two or more texts from the same period treat similar themes or topics.
>
> Analyze multiple interpretations of a story, drama, or poem (e.g., recorded or live production of a play or recorded novel or poetry), evaluating how each version interprets the source text. (Include at least one play by Shakespeare and one play by an American dramatist.)

Second, the Common Core document also provides a grade-level list in Appendix B of titles. The list shows a desired range of reading levels at each grade level which increase in complexity from grade 1 to grade 12. The list doesn't indicate the reading level of these titles according to a commonly used readability formula, nor are the titles required. They simply exemplify the range of complex texts desired at a particular grade level.

English Teachers are urged to use their own judgment as well as quantitative measures (i.e., a readability formula) when selecting specific titles for their classroom curriculum. In the absence of clear goals and guidelines for a coherent literature curriculum, this flexibility may ultimately mean little increase overall in the difficulty level of what most students now read in high school. It is too early to tell. There is nothing in the specifications for the common tests in the English language arts that points to a more demanding literature curriculum than most students now have.

CONCLUDING REMARKS

In the name of race, ethnicity, or gender identity, easier-to-read and often poorly written works have replaced many of the challenging works that had long been in the literature curriculum at each secondary grade level. The themes of these easier-to-read texts (e.g., xenophobia) might be difficult for many students to grasp but not their language and vocabulary.

In the absence of unpoliticized guidance from consultants and advisers, educational publishers could not help schools to maintain (or reconstruct) a coherent literature curriculum once the major characters' race, ethnicity, or gender came to be seen as the basis for choosing a literary work. It is not possible to work out a rationally sequenced course of literary study that links progressively more difficult works over the course of a grade and/or from grade to grade in intellectually and/or aesthetically defensible ways if there are nonliterary constraints imposed on publishers.

Works with high readability levels in the pre-World War II literature curriculum could have been replaced by comparably difficult literary works by members of non-European cultures or racial or ethnic groups in this country for students in standard or honors courses. Why they weren't recommended by English educators in their methods courses or leading professionals remains to be explained. Most high school students in the broad middle were once sufficiently able to read advanced texts and should have had their cultural horizons broadened by works whose vocabulary, syntax, and literary features were appropriately challenging.

POINTS TO REMEMBER

1. An incoherent literature curriculum caused initially by structural changes (conversion of year-long courses into semester electives and junior high schools into middle schools) to encourage more reading by lower-performing or unmotivated students slowed down the intellectual growth of the middle third of high school students (those motivated to stay in school until graduation). There is no evidence to suggest these reforms served to motivate unmotivated students.

2. These structural changes led to the abandonment of substantive academic goals in the English curriculum. They contributed to the ease with which easier-to-read, contemporary texts were added to the high school literature curriculum and to the extensive use of elementary level texts in the middle school literature curriculum.

3. Most states' standards and institutions of higher education have provided no useful guidelines on what literary texts, literary traditions, literary movements, or literary knowledge high school graduates or incoming college freshmen should be familiar with.

NOTES

1. http://englishcompanion.ning.com/forum/topics/the-stotsky-study-of-high?unfollow=1&xg_source=msg_com_forum.

2. James Moffett, *Teaching the Universe of Discourse* (Boston: Houghton Mifflin, 1968). See Chapter Four—Narrative: What Happened.

3. Stotsky, *Literary Study in Arkansas*, 37–41.

4. Allison Skerrett, "Of Literary Import: A Case of Cross-National Similarities in the Secondary English Curriculum in the United States and Canada," *Research in the Teaching of English,* 2010, 45 (1): 36–58.

5. Stotsky, *Literary Study in Arkansas*, 37–39.

7

How Two Learning Theories
Further Cripple Literary Study

The literature curriculum experienced by most high school students in standard or honors courses is dysfunctional in several ways. First, it is likely to be incoherent, meaning that whatever they are assigned to read does not connect to previous or subsequent readings in ways that cumulatively build literary or nonliterary knowledge or insights. Second, their curriculum consists of titles that overall do not increase in reading difficulty from grade to grade. While reading assignments may become more complex in theme, plot, character development, and point of view, there are overall no meaningful increases in the reading level of the text—its vocabulary difficulty and sentence complexity.

The third source of a dysfunctional literature curriculum lies in teachers' preferred approaches to literary study. English teachers more frequently use nonanalytical approaches to understand and interpret a work (e.g., a personal response or a focus on the work's historical, cultural, or biographical context) than close reading, or a careful analysis of the work itself. And the pedagogical approaches they frequently use inherently limit students' intellectual growth, even if a coherent and progressively demanding literature curriculum were in place.

After briefly profiling the major changes in instructional approaches to literary study over the past century, this chapter describes the two major learning theories promulgated in education schools that influence English teachers' approaches and explains their intellectual limitations. It then shows their application to literary study in a nationally known literature anthology so that it is clearer what the pedagogical counterparts of these learning theories mean in practice.

CHANGES IN APPROACHES TO
LITERARY STUDY AT THE SECONDARY LEVEL

Information on teachers' preferred approaches comes from their responses on the 2010 national literature survey to a question asking them to indicate what "might best describe your approach (es)" to teaching imaginative literature or literary nonfiction. Teachers could choose one or all of the dominant approaches employed or developed since literary study became part of the secondary curriculum in the late nineteenth century. Teachers' use of these approaches depends on their academic experiences and pedagogical training.

What are these approaches? From the late 1800s until roughly the 1940s, a literary work was placed within a biographical/historical context and seen chiefly as an embodiment of contemporary views of literary excellence and significant ideas, with its meaning a matter of personal impression. An approach called the "New Criticism" began in the 1930s and became dominant in the 1940s. Holding sway for about three decades, the New Criticism stressed analysis of the relationship between a work's form and its meaning. It was, as literary critic John Crowe Ransom described it in 1941, "a more objective criticism focusing on the intrinsic qualities of a work rather than on its biographical or historical contexts."[1]

A reaction to what some perceived as a narrow approach to literary study developed in the 1960s and 1970s under the rubric of reader response. Reader response approaches gained dominance over the New Criticism, stimulated in large part by Louise Rosenblatt's *Literature as Exploration*, first published in 1938. It served to launch the notion that the reader "creates the text" or "coauthors the literary work," encouraging teachers to ground the interpretation of a literary work in students' personal experiences or idiosyncratic responses to it.[2]

In the last third of the twentieth century, other approaches came into play that again sought to ground the interpretation of a literary work in its historical and cultural context, but this time emphasizing the author's race, ethnicity, gender, and biography, or the experiences of the group with which an author was identified (as in a multicultural approach). Among these late-twentieth-century approaches, a common thread was a general belief that the meaning of a literary work is undecidable—that its interpretation is open to a variety of possibilities.

Teachers' responses about their approach to literary study show all these approaches, including close reading, represented across classrooms (Tables 5 and 6 in Chapter Two). But close reading is slighted at each grade level in favor of a contextual approach or a personal response, even for nonfiction.

Common sense suggests that engaging students in a careful reading of a nonfiction text does not preclude asking them to locate historical, cultural, or biographical information that would deepen their understanding of that text. Biographical or other contextual materials may usefully supplement a close reading of either an imaginative or nonfiction text (e.g., by introducing the seminal ideas of the author's time).

Nevertheless, many students are being mistaught how to read nonfiction as well as poetry, drama, or fiction because of the influence of two different learning theories on the pedagogy used for literary study. These theories dominate their preparation programs, the textbooks they use, their professional development, and the research they are told is authoritative.

TWO LEARNING THEORIES DRIVING
PEDAGOGY IN THE LITERATURE CURRICULUM

Two different ideas about learning drive most of the pedagogy promoted in education schools today: constructivism and critical pedagogy. Although the label of "theory" is frequently applied to each of these concepts, neither is a learning theory in the way that scientifically-oriented researchers use the term—as an evidence-related explanation of something that can be observed and independently confirmed in the real world. Neither of these theories, as reflected in the pedagogical strategies derived from them, is supported by a known body of evidence.[3]

Proponents of these two ideas are concerned with the motivation to learn, especially the motivation of the lowest-achieving students in our public schools. They are much less concerned with academic outcomes.

Because of their focus on student engagement, their ideas have profoundly affected the literature curriculum and the learning process, and in contradictory ways.

Constructivism

One theory, often called constructivism, assumes that motivation to learn is enhanced by the opportunity to choose what to learn and how to learn it. This theory claims that what students try to learn must be constructed from their own initiatives and experiences. Meaningful learning is said to take place only when students have constructed their own understanding of the world they live in, whether from personal experience, their peers, or the texts they choose to read.

Constructivist educators believe that students will learn best not by being told what to learn, what something means, or what the answer to a problem is, but by pursuing their own questions about a phenomenon, using a hands-on, trial and error approach, making their own inferences and discoveries, and coming to their own conclusions. Constructivist educators deny that knowledge can be taught in the commonly understood meaning of "teach." Rather, they believe that only self-"discovered" academic knowledge can be truly learned and remembered.[4]

A reader response approach is the pedagogical counterpart of this learning theory for literary study—how to teach students to read a literary text. The teaching strategies favored by those who believe in this approach include peer-led small group work and student-selected reading and/or writing. (These might more accurately be called pseudo-teaching strategies.) In its radical form, strategies related to this approach encourage students to interpret what they read through the lens of personal or peer experience, even if their experience shapes an interpretation that may have little to do with what the author wrote. Any interpretation of a text can be considered valid in a radical approach.

According to Irma DeFord, an English teacher who spent twenty-eight years in a junior high school classroom, the approach relies on personal anecdote as a point of entry into imaginative prose. She believes that it teaches students little else "except how to identify with the characters and plot so they recognize themselves, their problems, and their own life experiences in a text."[5]

The use of reader response approaches by several generations of English teachers has had consequences. One example of the long-term influence of this pedagogy is the perceived inability of college freshmen to "argue" about what is in a text in their literature courses. According to Gerald Graff, professor of English and education at the University of Illinois at Chicago, the unmotivated, uncomprehending students overwhelming college English classrooms have not been taught how to summarize what they read and make arguments about it—the "name of the game in academe."[6] Graff does not try to explain why they have not been taught to do this, but Thomas Carnicelli does.[7]

For many years the Director of the English Teaching Major at the University of New Hampshire as well as a professor of English, Carnicelli sees incoming freshmen lacking in "traditional literacy." In his view, the effort to get "reluctant or indifferent students to read literature" has led to a problem that is "just as bad: the widespread acceptance of a literary theory that can undermine the value of reading literature in the first place." The theory to which he refers is the reader response approach, which he does not consider "a viable basis for teaching literature in a useful and responsible way:"

> It provides no clear standard of validity for either teachers or students. It gives the teacher no clear basis of authority: how is the teacher to direct a class discussion or grade a paper if all responses are equal? Finally, it undermines the whole purpose of having students read literature in the first place: to learn new perspectives on human experience. How can students learn anything from literary texts if they do not pay careful attention to what the authors have to say (p. 226)?

Given such criticisms, how did reader response approaches spread so far from their origins at the post-secondary level and become dominant in K–12? One cannot discount the influence of literature professors who used this approach in college classes attended by students intending to become secondary English teachers. Nor can one discount the influence of English education faculty in methods classes for prospective English teachers. Nor should one discount the influence of state standards in the English language arts as well as professional development programs for teachers designed to reflect what was in their methods courses or a state's standards.

Many state standards for the English language arts expressed a constructivist perspective. Could college freshmen argue about any one interpretation of a literary or non-literary text if they had been taught for twelve years to "respond to literary works on the basis of personal insights and respect the different responses of others" (a K–12 Montana standard) or "understand that a single text will elicit a wide variety of responses, each of which is valid from a personal, subjective perspective" (a K–12 Delaware standard)?[8]

Much depends on the version of a reader response approach their English teachers chose to use for literary study and how much close reading they built in. But it is not surprising that college instructors have found students paying little attention to a text to ensure their opinions were based on something in that text.

Social Justice and Critical Pedagogy

The other learning theory may be more familiar when described as a social justice approach to teaching and learning. This theory assumes that motivation to learn is enhanced by developing students' awareness of the historical and current grievances that social groups considered "oppressed" should hold against those who are to be perceived as their "oppressors." To implement this theory, teachers discredit traditional curricula (chiefly on the grounds that they reflect what "oppressors" want taught) and dwell on injustices done to the "oppressed," cultivate students' identity either as members of an "oppressed" group or as members of the "oppressor" group, and motivate them to political action of some kind.

A social justice theory is associated with a school of thought called "critical pedagogy." Wikipedia offers a clear and accurate definition of critical pedagogy: "Critical pedagogy is a teaching approach that attempts to help students question and challenge domination, and the beliefs and practices that dominate. It is a theory and practice of helping students achieve 'critical consciousness'—a state of understanding about the world that helps to liberate them from oppression."

The basic concepts of critical pedagogy were popularized by Paulo Freire in *Pedagogy for the Oppressed*, first published in English in 1970. A Brazilian educator, a Marxist, and judged one of the most influential educators of the twentieth century, Freire denigrated traditional curriculum content as oppressive. He also denigrated the pedagogy that he associated with it as a "banking concept of education" in which teachers "deposit" this oppressive knowledge into the minds of passive students.

Although Freire's ideas were aimed at the education of uneducated adults in Brazil—mostly illiterate farmers and fishermen—they spread through the educational world like wildfire, starting with post-secondary developmental reading and writing programs and then to all educational levels. It did not seem to matter to his acolytes that his ideas did not apply to K–12 or address the needs of small undereducated minorities in an industrialized and literate country.

Freire described teaching, or education in general, as a political act. He made no bones about it. After the 1960s, a more receptive audience could not be found than among college instructors and others involved in ethnic studies programs in this country.

To implement Freire's ideas, teachers eagerly sought to develop their students' political attitudes—group solidarity in students belonging to "non-dominant" social groups and hostility or resentment towards their "oppressors"—and to arouse them for political action based on their particular group identity.[9] Motivating adoption of critical pedagogy in part was the belief that low academic achievement in these non-dominant groups could be traced to a lack of motivation for, or resistance to, the cultural content and pedagogy of a curriculum that was not originally designed for them—thereby an alien and oppressive curriculum.

How effective have Freire's educational ideas been with respect to student achievement? Not surprisingly, there are no independent evaluations of his work, in Brazil or elsewhere, that attest to the efficacy of his ideas at any educational level and for any group of students.[10] His influence rests simply on passionate political faith, making it impossible to find teacher educators and their teacher followers in this country willing to articulate their own critical reflections on the educational value of the Freirean pedagogy they used with their students.

Critical pedagogy has strongly influenced the teaching of history in K–12, accelerating its absorption into the social studies with a stress on the academic trinity of race, ethnicity, and gender, and occasioning many local and national debates on what history American students should study. Whether called multicultural education or "culturally responsive education," critical pedagogy has also had a deep effect on literary study in the secondary grades. It has altered what students understand as American literature, as well as how they are to view the people and culture of the country they live in.

Yet, unlike the many national debates on American and world history, one searches in vain to find articles (positive, skeptical, or negative) by English teachers about the reach of critical pedagogy into the secondary literature curriculum. This phenomenon—the absence of comment—raises questions about professional intimidation.[11]

Like the constructivists, advocates of critical pedagogy are not interested in the teaching of literary appreciation or analytical reading. Unlike the constructivists, they want teachers to guide classroom "dialogue" and reading materials with a heavy hand.[12] They eschew student choice in what is read in favor of teacher choice of reading materials in order to contextualize the social or political issues they have linked to the chosen titles. Moreover, because the content of these contextual materials is apt to be as new to high school students as the work is, this means that the teacher's use of them in the classroom is more likely didactic than analytic.

How strong an influence does critical pedagogy have in our education schools? Although few teacher educators describe themselves as critical pedagogues, David Labaree, professor of education at Stanford University, stresses that "education schools are solidly in the progressive camp ideologically," encouraging educators, among other things, to promote "values of community, cooperation, tolerance, justice, and democratic equality" and to engage students in projects that "integrate the disciplines around socially relevant themes."[13]

HOW THESE THEORIES INFLUENCE LITERARY
STUDY AND THE SCHOOL'S CIVIC MISSION

A pedagogy based on social justice began to influence the secondary literature curriculum in the 1980s after multicultural texts had streamed into the reading and English curriculum. The two movements merged when it became clear that each facilitated the other. The social and political criteria that multiculturalism justified helped to determine the literary works read in the English class *and* the thematic connections that teachers encouraged students to see among these works. They also motivated use of other kinds of material as well—videos, diaries, letters, and a variety of other primary documents—as Chapter Five shows.[14]

Examples from the 2000 edition of McDougal Littell's grade 11 anthology of American literature show how a social justice-oriented pedagogy has captured a constructivist pedagogy to shape what students read in a literature textbook and how teachers are advised to approach its goals. It should be noted that not only was this anthology approved for adoption in textbook adoption states, it was also the anthology that the University of California chose to feature in its online pilot course for a grade 11 course in American literature in 2004.

On what basis might the pedagogical apparatus in this anthology be seen as authoritative in the field and a reflection of what is promoted in English education coursework? To begin with, most of its eight authors are nationally known professors in English education. Two authors have co-directed the federally funded National Research Center for Literature Teaching and Learning at the University of Albany—SUNY since 1987. In addition, the introduction clearly indicates the major role these eight professors played in the development of the 2000 edition. They guided its "conceptual development," "participated actively in shaping prototype materials for major components," and "reviewed completed prototypes and/or completed units to ensure consistency with current research and the philosophy of the series."

A back-breaking 1400 pages long, with over 160 excerpts and complete selections from a variety of genres, the organization of the anthology reflects a social studies approach. That is, current social and political issues are used to organize historical content in the anthology's seven units.

The result of a social studies approach is that contemporary selections addressing the constructs of race, ethnicity, and gender cast a heavy presentistic shadow on the older selections with which they are thematically grouped. Not only have many readings chosen for their thematic relevance been lifted out of their historical context (e.g., Arthur Miller's play *The Crucible* is offered in the unit on the Puritans), many literary offerings also have been chosen for the political uses that could be made of them (e.g., Dwight Okita's poem on the Japanese-American internment or Denise Levertov's poem on a demonstration against the Vietnam War).

The goals of critical pedagogy are embedded in the pedagogical structure for individual selections in the student text (ST) and the teacher edition

(TE). In the ST, this structure typically consists of background information for the selection, a suggested focus for reading it, post-selection questions to stimulate connections to their lives and "check comprehension," questions to prompt students to "think critically" about the selection, questions to help students "extend" their interpretation of the selection by making further connections to their lives and comparisons with other selections, and biographical material on the author. The questions asking students to make links to their lives reflect a constructivist pedagogy. They are invariably superseded by questions to "think critically."

"Thinking critically," "critical thinking," and critical pedagogy do not mean teaching students to be skeptical. They do not refer to analytical thinking or doing a "critique," an analysis of strengths and weaknesses, or positive and negative features of something. Critical pedagogy and critical thinking mean thinking negatively about the larger society one lives in. What might the results of "thinking critically" be, using this anthology? If teachers draw faithfully on the pedagogical apparatus in the student text and teacher edition, students are likely to have formed negative judgments about (1) the worth of this country's existence as a nation, (2) the extent of its internal cohesion historically and today, (3) the character of the men who articulated its founding political principles, (4) the validity of the popular images and metaphors used to describe this country's cultural traits, and (5) the character of those inhabitants who express its dominant cultural values.

How does the pedagogical apparatus lead teachers towards the goals of critical pedagogy? In the TE, the editors provide teachers with very specific "possible responses" to the discussion questions in the ST, additional questions for class discussion, and different kinds of literary and historical information to use. Through the "possible responses" and other material in the TE, teachers learn how to guide students to think "critically" or "extend" their interpretations so that both teachers and students arrive at the right critical thoughts and interpretations. The examples below show different ways the pedagogical apparatus subtly cultivates anticivic, anti-Christian, and antifamily attitudes throughout the anthology.

Titles of Major Units Convey an Anti-Civic Viewpoint

Selections are grouped in seven units, ranging from pre-1620 "Origins and Encounters," with two parts titled "In Harmony with Nature" and

"Exploration and Exploitation," to post-1940 "War Abroad and Conflict at Home," the second part of which is titled "Integration and Disintegration." The latter title takes us to the present, leaving students with the notion that we are a people no longer united around anything.

Questions in the ST or TE Frequently Invite Invidious Comparisons across Groups or Time to Reinforce Understanding that this Country was Illegitimately Conceived

E.g., selections in the first unit highlight European exploitation or brutality in the New World in the context of selections about the cultural traditions of several Indian tribes, their hospitality to the first Europeans they encountered, and the slave trade. Students are asked to compare the "experiences of captured Africans brought to North America on slave ships with the experiences of the Pilgrims or Cabeza de Vaca's men" (p. 98). The TE notes that "students should understand that the major difference between the experiences of African slaves and those of Pilgrims is that the Pilgrims chose to make their journey" (p. 98).

Wanting no sympathy for Pilgrims or Puritans, the ST cleverly implies a contemporary analogy to discredit them, commenting that the Puritans "used the Bible to justify their occupation of the land and their use of force against Native Americans." In other words, New England can be viewed historically as "occupied territory" overtaken by a group of Bible-toting religious zealots.

E.g., after an excerpt from a travelogue by William Least Heat-Moon, students are asked to compare the "experiences and attitudes of William Least Heat-Moon, William Bradford, and Alvar Nunez Cabeza de Vaca as they explored America." The TE suggests: "William Least Heat-Moon has a greater respect for and interest in Native American culture. Bradford and de Vaca are wary of Native Americans, regarding them as barbarians whose way of life is inferior to Western European culture" (p. 107).

White Americans Tend to be Portrayed as Ugly Racists

E.g., after a selection by William Least Heat-Moon, students are asked "What do you think makes it difficult to be a Hopi?" and are given the following points to address: "how most whites view Native Americans, how some Native Americans view others for 'acting like Anglos,' and how the Hopi and other Native Americans have historically been treated" (p. 107). The TE suggests that "it is difficult to be a Hopi because many whites are prejudiced against Native Americans; others tend to idealize them, denying their humanity. Some Native Americans disparage others for adopting Anglo ways. Furthermore, the Hopi and other Native Americans have long been treated as foreigners, not citizens" (p. 107).

E.g., the TE itself describes a long selection titled "The Legend of Gregorio Cortez" by Americo Paredes in the unit on the settlement of the west as follows: "The narration reveals deep conflicts between the two cultures—Anglo and Mexican. The sheriffs and rangers are portrayed as bullying racists so inept that hundreds of them cannot capture one man. The American horse trader spews demeaning stereotypes. Cortez is harassed and receives no justice in the U.S. courts" (p. 718). One cannot help but conjecture that this selection was chosen precisely because it is so rich in politically correct stereotypes.

E.g., the last unit in the anthology, covering from 1940 to the present, offers a story, "Armistice," by Bernard Malamud. The story takes place in 1940 in Brooklyn in the context of the imminent surrender of the French to the Nazis in Europe and focuses on the interactions between a Jewish immigrant grocer and one of his suppliers, who is portrayed as sympathetic to the Nazis and an anti-Semite. The supplier describes himself as a "hundred percent American" (p. 1081). Here, too, one cannot help but wonder if this character's self-description was the reason that the story was selected for the anthology.

Selections Facilitate a Stereotype of Christians as Hypocrites or Bigots

E.g., after a selection by Olaudah Equiano on the Middle Passage, students are asked: "Who do you think are the 'nominal Christians' that Equiano refers to in the last paragraph? Do you agree with his epithet? Support your answer with evidence from the selection" (p. 98). The TE suggests: "Equiano is talking about people who practice slavery yet claim to be guided by Christian values—Christians in name only. Most students will agree that holding human beings as slaves is not morally acceptable behavior" (p. 98). Here we see how difficult it would be for students not to agree to the last statement and then deny that Christians in fact are hypocrites.

E.g., after Arthur Miller's play *The Crucible*, the TE suggests staging a Mock Trial in which students might try "Reverend Parris for his
involvement in the conviction of innocent people..." (p. 235). Explaining
"irony" as a literary technique, the TE suggests asking students "what is
ironic about the entire premise of the witch trials." "Possible Response:
All the accusers called themselves Puritans, and yet they lied and gave
false testimonies—sins in the Bible. The people who were wrongly ac-
cused were also Puritans, and they tried to tell the truth—something required by the Bible—and they were hanged for it. Finally, the authorities,
who were supposed to follow the Bible and rational principles of justice,
did the exact opposite and condoned the killing of innocent people. The
Salem witch trials occurred in the name of Christianity, and yet these trials embodied the very sins that Christianity condemns" (p. 242). By the
time students have finished early American history, it would be unlikely
for them to view Christianity, individual Christians, or anyone else who
believes in the Bible positively.

The TE Ignores Well-Known Positive Facts

E.g., in the historical background to the Civil War, the TE presents no
information on the abolition by the British of slavery and the trans-Atlan-
tic slave trade. Nor is the role of white abolitionists apparent in the unit on
the Civil War, which offers only one selection by a white abolitionist—a
poem by James Russell Lowell.

The ST Suggests that No One Should Want to Assimilate to this Country's Values

E.g., in its introduction to Walt Whitman's poems, the ST indicates:
"Most of his poems are marked by optimism, vitality, and a love of nature, free expression, and democracy—values often associated with the
America of his day" (p. 396). The inference to be drawn is that these
values cannot be associated with America today, and, indeed, students are
asked later to address this question.

E.g., after selections that debunk the American dream and portray
America as little more than a nation of greedy bigots, the TE suggests that
students prepare an argument about assimilation. "Outline an argument for

or against assimilation—the process of adapting one's values and expectations in order to fit into the prevailing society. Keep in mind issues such as cultural identity, personal integrity, and economic necessity..." (p. 893). Forewarned that personal integrity is at stake, what student would see assimilation as desirable?

Selections Have an Anti-Marriage, Anti-Family Theme

The anthology wants teachers and students to understand that American women have been oppressed by their husbands and society at large throughout their country's history, that marriage is an oppressive institution that has caused women much suffering, that middle-class American family life leaves much to be desired, and that women have achieved a great deal despite marital, social, and political oppression. The anthology also tries to show that they are, in fact, superior to men in some ways.

E.g., students are asked: "What influences from the *Declaration of Independence* do you see on Olympe de Gouges' *Declaration of the Rights of Women*? How do the two documents differ?" (p. 279). The TE suggests: "One difference is that Jefferson cites specific grievances against George III to justify the decisive step taken by the colonists. Olympe de Gouges, on the other hand, reasons from general principles—for instance, that people subject to the law must also be allowed to express their views freely."

Using a relatively unknown selection, the TE wants teachers to comment on a woman thinking at a higher level than Jefferson did in composing the *Declaration of Independence*, and to imply that women are superior to men. The "stereotype" being attacked here, of course, is that men think from general principles while women think at the lower level of detail.

E.g., before students read Charlotte Gilman Perkins's "The Yellow Wallpaper," the TE indicates that the story is "an example of the new literature that began to emerge in the late 1880s, in which long-repressed women's voices began to be heard. Women's lives were ruled by their husbands and by their perceived place in society" (p. 765). The TE does not explain why there are so many exceptions to this generalization, such as Abigail Adams, Harriet Beecher Stowe, Louisa May Alcott, and Susan B. Anthony.

E.g., "The Yellow Wallpaper" is followed by Kate Chopin's "The Story of an Hour," which is described in the TE as follows: "[It] reveals the innermost thoughts of a woman who is told that her husband has suddenly been killed. Her thoughts and feelings about her new-found freedom give insights about women's lives at the end of the nineteenth century." (At the end of the story, she drops dead of a heart attack when she discovers her husband had not been killed, after all.)

After students read Kate Chopin's "The Story of an Hour," students are asked: "How would you compare the themes of the two stories? Which story do you prefer, and why?" Possible responses in the TE: "Chopin's story is shorter than Gilman's, but its sentences tend to be longer. Its narrator is objective and uses the third-person point of view, as opposed to the highly subjective first-person point of view in "The Yellow Wallpaper. Both stories show upper-middle class married women of the 1890s trapped in confining roles and escaping through tragedy—death in one case, insanity in the other. Have students explain their preferences" (p. 786). This suggestion is almost ludicrous. Why should students be asked to choose between these two stories' themes? Why wasn't a story about a woman of achievement included?

E.g., to make sure teachers and students have absorbed the right understandings from these stories, students are asked in a unit wrap-up: "What do you feel you've learned about the social position of American women in the past? What new thoughts do you have about the American dream?" The ST goes on to say: "Many of the selections in the first part of the unit show American women's struggles with social constraints, stereotypes, and inequalities. Review the ways in which the female characters in these selections respond to oppression or limitation. Which character did you find it easiest to identify with? Which character did you find it most difficult to identify with?"

The ST also says: "Think about the American dream in relation to the selections in the second part of this unit. Which characters would classify the American dream as an illusion? Which would view it as a reality?" (p. 910). Given the selections offered, very few would view it as a reality.

E.g., in a unit titled "Alienation of the Individual," after a poem by Anne Sexton that follows one by Sylvia Plath, students are asked: "Based on the details you recorded (in your notebook), expand the title ("Self in 1958") into a general statement that explains the theme, or main idea, of the poem." The TE suggests: "the idealized role of the 1950s homemaker left many feeling alienated and not real" (p. 1061). Their biographies inform students that both women committed suicide at relatively young ages.

E.g., the TE suggests that teachers ask students to respond to a quotation on "America's middle class" in the ST from *The Organization Man* by William A. Whyte Jr. that appears in the historical background for Unit Seven, Integration and Disintegration in Postwar Society. Possible response: "He implies that those Americans, usually men, who strive for the American dream by working for big business become totally removed from their families" (p. 1133).

E.g., Anne Tyler is described as someone who looks at "the loneliness and isolation of middle class family life" today, and her story "Teenage Wasteland" is about a boy who finally runs away from home and never returns to his "controlling and accusatory" parents (p. 1168). Tyler's story is followed by "Separating," a short story by John Updike about an upper-middle class couple with four children who have decided to separate. The ST asks students to think of "some reasons that married couples separate? How do you think a wife and a husband feel once they have decided to separate? If they have children, how do you think the children feel?" (p. 1181).

Positive Views of American Cultural Values or Traits Are Debunked

E.g., Unit Three, on nineteenth-century American literature, is titled "The Spirit of Individualism." The first section of the unit, titled "Celebration of Self," presents the Transcendental optimists Emerson, Thoreau, and Whitman. The second section presents Poe, Hawthorne, and Melville (writers who are usually characterized as anti-Transcendental pessimists) in a section titled "The Dark Side of Individualism." This misleading title not only leaves students without a clear grasp of the real dark side of celebrating the self—the preoccupations of obsessed or tormented individuals as portrayed by the anti-Transcendental pessimists—but also serves to negativize the concept of individualism itself, a political and cultural philosophy positively associated with this country.

E.g., after Edward Arlington Robinson's poems "Miniver Cheevy" and "Richard Cory," students are asked: "How would you relate "Miniver

Cheevy" and "Richard Cory" to the American dream? Possible response in the TE: "Both poems illustrate the failure of the "American dream": Richard Cory seems to be the embodiment of that dream, yet he chooses to kill himself; Miniver Cheevy rejects the idea of an American dream, focusing instead on an idealized past to justify his own failures" (p. 832).

E.g., the TE explains that two poems by Paul Laurence Dunbar "both demonstrate that the American dream is not a reality for all Americans. People who can achieve the dream may have the illusion that it is open to everyone, but those whose dreams are caged like a bird have a different perspective" (p. 834).

E.g., the TE explains that in a short story "In the American Society" by Chinese American writer Gish Jen on how "one immigrant family aspires to their version of the American Dream," their "illusions that material success will guarantee social privilege are dashed by a suburban society whose reality is inherently racist" (p. 877). Later the TE suggests that teachers "tell students that this story takes place in the 1960s, when racism was a serious issue that the nation was just beginning to address. Many private country clubs denied admission to Jews or to anyone who wasn't white and preferably an Anglo-Saxon Protestant as well" (p. 882).

Summary

Because most K–12 textbooks purchased for class use are first vetted by large groups of teachers and others, especially in adoption states, a K–12 textbook must not easily appear to be suggesting a "critical" pedagogy through its pedagogical apparatus. Thus, many first-rate selections appear in this 1400-page McDougal Littell anthology.

But there is almost no humor or irreverence (e.g., no Will Rogers sayings or a Mark Twain satire), an outstanding feature of American literature. There are few selections that will appeal to boys or help to socialize them, that is, nothing to suggest the positive energy invested in exploration, ingenuity, or resourcefulness (such as Benjamin Franklin's autobiography), no selections showing older mating or courtship patterns (such as "The Courtship of Miles Standish"), no selections showing a healthy family structure, no selections highlighting this country's political values in times of danger or war (such as a FDR Fireside Chat or a piece of historical nonfiction about World War II or 9/11).

The teaching apparatus in McDougal Littell's grade 11 anthology of American literature helps students to see that Original Sin lies not in man but in the nation's founding and cultural values. The teacher's task is to help students understand who the victims of social injustice have been and what social, political, economic, and religious forces have oppressed them. It clearly does not give American Protestantism the serious attention it warrants in a literature course, leaving American students unable to understand why the Framers were skeptics, not utopians, and the profound difference that made to American history.

Howard Mumford Jones, for many years an English professor at Harvard University, articulated concerns in *Jeffersonianism and the American Novel* about whether the civic character needed for representative self-government had been undermined by this country's major writers.[15] In our political culture, he observed, the adult American is understood to be "a being capable of both rational and moral choice." Upon this assumption, he wrote, "the republic rests."

Yet, as he pointed out in his survey of American novels of the twentieth century, they have seriously weakened, if not obliterated, a view of the individual as someone free to make choices and then to be responsible for the choices they made. Jones could not have anticipated that teaching strategies derived from a learning theory about social justice would supply the coup de grace in secondary English classes.

CONCLUDING REMARKS

David Labaree tries to make the case that education schools have "no ability to promote progressive practices in the schools" or to control public education. Yet, the contents of a leading grade 11 American literature anthology suggest how real though subtle their control of public education is. Indeed, leading education school faculty shape every subject taught in the schools at every grade level through their control, direct or indirect, of the content and pedagogy in the textbooks used in our public schools, the coursework in teachers' training programs, and their professional development programs.

The decline in reading achievement and in literary reading may be partly accounted for by the two learning theories and their pedagogical counterparts that education school faculty have promulgated to shape the English curriculum, classroom instruction, and student learning. The classroom application of either theory deals a lethal blow to pedagogy seeking to cultivate the pleasures and uses of the imagination. Together, they effectively bury it.

They also cripple young adolescents' intellectual development. Students fail to learn how to think critically, or analytically, because the literature class has been turned into a mock social studies or sociology class with an agenda. They also fail to learn how to read carefully any kind of text. A stress on personal response or biographical materials does not replace the need to teach students how to read the text itself. As Paul Cantor, an English professor at the University of Virginia, observes: "If you really want to learn something about Shakespeare, go back to the plays—that is where his wisdom is to be found and not in any account of the details of his evidently rather ordinary life."[16]

POINTS TO REMEMBER

1. Two learning theories and their pedagogical counterparts dominate instruction in professional preparation programs and professional development programs for teachers.

2. Neither constructivism or social justice/critical pedagogy has evidence to show that it promotes the academic achievement of any group of students.

3. Together these two theories and their pedagogical counterparts negatively influence what is in a literature program and how literature is taught.

NOTES

1. Ransom, J.C., *The New Criticism* (Norfolk, CT: New Directions, 1941).

2. See, for example, S. Justman, "Bibliotherapy: Literature as Exploration Reconsidered," *Academic Questions*, 2010, 23: 125–135.

3. Constructivists claim that in studies where children were compared on higher-order thinking skills, constructivist students seemed to outperform their peers. But it is impossible to find out what these studies are and what the experimenters actually did. According to P.A. Kirschner, J. Sweller, and R. E. Clark,

"Why Minimal Guidance during Instruction Does Not Work: An Analysis of the Failure of Constructivist, Discovery, Problem-Based, Experiential, and Inquiry-Based Teaching"*Educational Psychologist* 2006, 41 (2): 75–86: "There appears no body of research supporting the technique. In so far as there is any evidence from controlled studies, it almost uniformly supports direct, strong instructional guidance rather than constructivist-based minimal guidance during the instruction of novice to intermediate learners. Even for students with considerable prior knowledge, strong guidance while learning is most often found to be equally effective as unguided approaches. Not only is unguided instruction normally less effective; there is also evidence that it may have negative results when student acquire misconceptions or incomplete or disorganized knowledge."

4. For a succinct and clear explanation of constructivism in science and mathematics education, see Michael R. Matthews, "Old Wine in New Bottles: A Problem with Constructivist Epistemology,"*Philosophy of Education*, 1992. http://www.ed.uiuc.edu/eps/PES-Yearbook/92_docs/Matthews.HTM.

5. Irma DeFord, "Why Students Resist Reading," *American School Board Journal*, 2004, 191: 18–19.

6. Gerald Graff, *Clueless in Academe: How Schooling Obscures the Life of the Mind* (New Haven: Yale University Press, 2004).

7. Thomas Carnicelli, "The English Language Arts in American Schools: Problems and Proposals," in *What's at Stake in the K–12 Standards Wars: A Primer for Educational Policy Makers*, ed. Sandra Stotsky (New York: Peter Lang, 2000), 211–236.

8. For more examples of pedagogically problematic standards, see Appendix C in Sandra Stotsky, *The State of State English Standards* (Washington D.C.: Thomas B. Fordham Institute, 2005).

9. For an example, see the mission statement and curriculum materials in the Mexican American Studies Program in the Tucson Public Schools, developed by university-level instructors.

10. For a critical evaluation of Freire-inspired programs in the United States and Puerto Rico, see http://www.bmartin.cc/dissent/documents/Facundo/Facundo.html.

11. I seem to have authored the few that can be found. See, for example, Sandra Stotsky, "The Changing Literature Curriculum in K–12," *Academic Questions*, 7 (1993–94): 1, 53-62; Sandra Stotsky, "The Transformation of Secondary School Literature Programs: Good News and Bad," *Phi Delta Kappan,* 1995, 76 (8): 605–612; Sandra Stotsky, "The State of Literary Study in National and State English Language Arts Standards: Why It Matters and What Can Be Done about It," in *What's at Stake in the K–12 Standards Wars: A Primer for Educational Policy Makers*, ed. Sandra Stotsky (New York: Peter Lang, 2000), 237–258.

12. For example, in *Literacy: Reading the Word and the World*, by Paulo Freire and Donaldo Macedo (Routledge & Kegan Paul,1987), Freire and Macedo offer no examples of true "dialogue." Freire's instructional material seems to consist of revolutionary slogans and Marxist propaganda.

13. David Labaree, "The Ed Schools' Romance with Progressivism," in *Brookings Papers on Education Policy* 2004, ed. Diane Ravitch (Washington, D.C.: Brookings Institution, 2004), 90–91.

14. Sandra Stotsky, "Anti-Civic Uses of Literary Discourse," in *Análisis del Discurso: Lengua, Cultura, Valores.* Actas del I Congreso Internacional, eds. Manuel Casado Velarde, Ramón González Ruiz, y Victoria Romero Gualda, Universidad de Navarra, Pamplona: Madrid, Arco/Libros, 2006, vol. I, 65–89. (ISBN de toda la obra: 84-7635-632-3)

15. Teachers College Press, 1966.

16. Paul Cantor, "Average Bill," review of *Shakespeare*, by Michael Wood, *Claremont Review of Books*, 2004, 4 (3): 66–70.

8

How to Create Coherent
Sequences of Informational Texts

There are many causes of the low state of civic literacy in the United Sates Among them: what is taught in college-level history or political science courses to undergraduates; what is taught in professional development for K–12 teachers; where the Founding Period is apt to be taught in K–12; and what those licensed to teach history may or may not know about American political principles and institutions. Regardless of cause, most students graduate from American public schools without the knowledge and skills they ought to have in order to be informed, responsible, and participating citizens at any level of government.

Common Core's literature and reading standards, just released in June 2010, were not intended as a solution for the dysfunctional or missing civics curricula in our schools, colleges, or teacher preparation and professional development programs.[1] They will, however, strongly influence what high school English teachers assign in the coming years. It therefore behooves educators in every school district in the country to use the civic content in Common Core's high school English standards to guide development of a coherent reading curriculum through the secondary grades. Such a curriculum could help to ensure that by the end of grade 12 students are both ready for college and able to read primary sources on the institutions, principles, and practices in this country's unique forms of self-government.

The purpose of this chapter is to show how several of Common Core's standards for English Language Arts and Literacy in History can serve as

clear guides to the development of a civically rich, intellectually demanding, and coherent literature curriculum using an approach known as backmapping. It will also explain why the most productive implementation
of these new standards should engage the collaboration of the political
science and English departments in a state's institutions of higher education with its teacher preparation and professional development programs.

THE STATE OF CIVIC LITERACY IN THE SCHOOLS

It is not hard to document the sorry state of civic literacy in American
public schools. Age, grade level, and source of information make no difference. The results and trends are consistent. For example, on the 2006 civics
test given by the National Assessment of Educational Progress (NAEP),
grade 12 scores (and grade 8 scores) were stagnant from 1998 to 2006.[2]

What did that mean with respect to basic civic literacy? As one example, just 43 percent of the grade 12 test-takers could describe the meaning
of federalism in American government, or the sharing of power between
the federal and state governments. This percentage alone suggests that the
K–12 curriculum does not have a strong impact on pre-college students'
understanding of this country's basic political institutions and principles.

The 2010 civics results released by NAEP in April 2011 were more de-
pressing.[3] Although the average score in 2010 for twelfth graders was not
significantly different from their average score in 1998, the NAEP survey
of what students are studying revealed serious and growing deficiencies
in the high school curriculum. The percentage of students who said they
studied the president and cabinet during the school year fell significantly
from 63 percent in 1998 to 59 percent in 2010, and the percentage of students who said they studied the U.S. Constitution during the school year
fell significantly from 72 percent in 2006 to 67 percent in 2010.

It is not clear why a smaller percentage of our students are studying
these topics as seniors. The score on the following open-ended question
alone suggests that the majority of grade 12 students have a limited or
poor understanding of this country. Students were asked first to read a
quotation from Israel Zangwill's play *The Melting Pot*, and then to define
the meaning of the term and comment on whether "melting pot" is appro-

priate to describe the United States. Only 35 percent of students received a "complete" rating on the two-part question.

Long-term voting trends in national elections for young adults suggest that a low level of civic literacy goes hand in glove with a low level of civic participation. Voter turnout among young American citizens (18 to 24) in the 2010 midterm election was 21.3 percent, declining almost steadily from 25.4 percent in 1974, according to estimates from the recently released 2010 U.S. Census Current Population Survey, November Supplement.[4]

CURRICULUM PLACEMENT PROBLEMS

The history of the Founding or the Constitutional Period appears to be disappearing from many undergraduate and graduate history curricula or professional development workshops for history teachers. The major exceptions generally have been those workshops funded by the National Endowment for the Humanities, the Center for Civic Education, and Traditional American History grants.[5]

Nevertheless, even if current history teachers have not studied the Founding Period in adequate depth in their own undergraduate education, its historical and philosophical background is often taught at grade levels where, a cynic might observe, in-depth understanding is not possible for most students and not necessary for the teacher. It may also be taught in ways that are unlikely to lead to an in-depth understanding.

Traditionally, many students have studied U.S. history and the Founding Period in grade 8, and many still do. The grade 8 placement is due in part to the theory behind the "spiral curriculum," a way of designing a K–12 curriculum that, when applied to the study of U.S. history, made some sense at the time it was proposed decades ago. Educators believed that it made little sense to teach U.S. history from 1492 to the present in each of grades 5, 8, and 11, the three years that might be devoted to national history, chiefly because students never got very far into the twentieth century at any grade level. So, proponents of the spiral curriculum suggested that grade 5 go from 1492 to the War of 1812, grade 8 from the Founding Period to Reconstruction after a review of the Revolutionary

War, and grade 11 from Reconstruction to the present after a review of the Founding Period.

The problem with grade 8 is that by default it may be where the most intensive study of the Founding in a historical context takes place unless the high school provides a U.S. history survey course in grade 11 that begins around 1620. Needless to say, if the grade at which students study the Founding Period is grade 8, it is unlikely that they will learn much if anything about the Enlightenment, John Locke, or Montesquieu, and read *The Federalist Papers*.

However, the Founding Period may be taught in U.S. government courses. Over half of the states now require such a course. So do many school districts in states that don't require it. It is usually a one-semester course in grade 12, although it may be taught as a civics course in grade 9.[6] In 2004, the most popular textbook for the U.S. Government course was Richard Remy's *United States Government: Democracy in Action*, published by Glencoe McGraw-Hill, far exceeding the old best seller, *Magruder's American Government*.[7] It includes chapters on the Founding Period, the Constitutional Convention, the English legal tradition, the Enlightenment era, and American colonial era antecedents to the Founding.

COMMON CORE'S READING STANDARDS

In 2010, a movement to develop national standards in basic subjects came to fruition. The National Governors Association and the Council of Chief State School Officers are credited with the joint development in a project titled "Common Core State Standards Initiative," a set of K–12 standards in mathematics and in the English language arts and reading. Enticed by the criteria in the U.S. Department of Education's Race to the Top competitive grants and encouraged by a variety of organizations heavily funded by the Bill and Melinda Gates Foundation, over forty-five states have adopted Common Core's standards.

It should not be forgotten that the precise title of Common Core's English language arts standards is Common Core State Standards for English Language Arts and Literacy in History/Social Studies, Science, and Technical Subjects. However, Common Core's document does not make it clear how English teachers can be held accountable for the teaching of literacy in history/social studies, science, and technical subjects on forthcoming national reading tests based on these standards.

The same question might be asked with respect to the grade 11/12 reading test given by the NAEP, which also requires 70 percent of the reading test items to focus on informational reading. However, because the NAEP tests by law cannot be used for accountability purposes, their results cause little local anxiety. Moreover, the NAEP tests are not given to all grade 12 students in every school but to only a representative sample. Nevertheless, while the content of the forthcoming national reading tests with respect to history and science is not yet clear, Common Core does expect teachers across the curriculum to teach students how to read and understand the textbooks and other reading materials they assign in their courses.

Common Core's Standards for English Language Arts come in two varieties: "college and career readiness standards" (CCRS), and grade-level standards. The CCRS for literary and informational reading are mostly generic skills drawn from David Conley's 2003 report "Understanding University Success," which presents "college readiness standards" for each major subject in the arts and sciences,[8] and surveys by American College Testing (ACT) during the 2000s.[9]

Common Core's College and Career Readiness Standards

Drawing from these sources and others like them, the committee appointed by the National Governors Association and the Council of Chief State School Officers to develop Common Core's standards came up with ten generic "College and Career Readiness Anchor Standards for Reading" (p. 35) listed below.[10] According to these organizations and all the experts and reports they drew on, when high school students can demonstrate their ability to apply these skills with proficiency to complex literary and informational texts, they can be considered ready for authentic college-level coursework.

1. Read closely to determine what the text says explicitly and to make logical inferences from it; cite specific textual evidence when writing or speaking to support conclusions drawn from the text.

2. Determine central ideas or themes of a text and analyze their development; summarize the key supporting details and ideas.
3. Analyze how and why individuals, events, and ideas develop and interact over the course of a text.
4. Interpret words and phrases as they are used in a text, including determining technical, connotative, and figurative meanings, and analyze how specific word choices shape meaning or tone.
5. Analyze the structure of texts, including how specific sentences, paragraphs, and larger portions of the text (e.g., a section, chapter, scene, or stanza) relate to each other and the whole.
6. Assess how point of view or purpose shapes the content and style of a text.
7. Integrate and evaluate content presented in diverse formats and media, including visually and quantitatively, as well as in words.
8. Delineate and evaluate the argument and specific claims in a text, including the validity of the reasoning as well as the relevance and sufficiency of the evidence.
9. Analyze how two or more texts address similar themes or topics in order to build knowledge or to compare the approaches the authors take.
10. Read and comprehend complex literary and informational texts independently and proficiently.

Purpose of the College and Career Readiness Standards

As comprehensive as these ten generic standards may seem to be, they are mainly skills and contain no cultural content. That is, they don't express intellectual objectives that could guide curriculum developers in working out progressively more challenging sequences of readings at the secondary level, either within a grade or from grade to grade.

Recognizing the need for "additional specificity" to help teachers and curriculum developers, Common Core also came up with grade-level standards from K–12. According to the standards writers, the CCRS and the grade-specific reading standards are "necessary complements...that together define the skills and understandings that all students must demonstrate."

It is in these grade-specific standards at the high school level that the endpoint, or the intellectual goals, for the English language arts curriculum can be found. The state of civic literacy in this country may be influenced by the content of two of Common Core's Reading Standards for Informational Text in grades 9–12:

For grades 9–10: Analyze seminal U.S. documents of historical and literary significance (e.g., Washington's "Farewell Address," the "Gettysburg Address," Roosevelt's "Four Freedoms" speech, King's "Letter from Birmingham Jail"), including how they address related themes and concepts.

For grades 11–12: Analyze seventeenth-, eighteenth-, and nineteenth-century foundational U.S. documents of historical and literary significance (including the *Declaration of Independence,* the *Preamble to the Constitution,* the *Bill of Rights,* and Lincoln's "Second Inaugural Address") for their themes, purposes, and rhetorical features.

English teachers are also to be held accountable for the following Literature standard:

For grades 11–12: Demonstrate knowledge of eighteenth-, nineteenth- and early-twentieth-century foundational works of American literature, including how two or more texts from the same period treat similar themes or topics.

As can be seen, the first two standards above expect students to understand the "purposes, rhetorical features, related themes, and concepts" in our seminal political documents. The third standard above expects students to understand foundational works of American literature in the past three centuries relating to these themes and topics. The focus of these particular standards is clearly on the content of what is in these seminal texts, not on students' affective responses to their content or on the iterative processes of writing and revising common to English classes in recent decades.

It is obvious that if high school students are to read and analyze the Founding documents specified for grades 11 and 12, they need to be familiar with the literary and historical context for these documents as well as their philosophical antecedents. While some contextual and antecedent information can be studied simultaneously with the reading of these documents, teachers will need to assign students grade-appropriate literary and informational texts from grade 6 to grade 10 to enable students to draw on familiar information when they first read these basic political documents in grade 11 or 12. Teachers will also have to build their capacity to read texts written at a time when educated citizens writing for the public used large vocabularies and wrote long and complex sentences.

How Their Intellectual and Civic Goals Can Guide Curriculum Developers

What more precisely would classroom teachers and curriculum developers need to take into account in order to identify particular texts students should be assigned in grades 6–10 in preparation for reading one particular seminal text? Let's start with an example that most people would agree all students should read before they graduate from an American high school—*The Federalist Papers*. (In fact, *The Federalist Papers* is the only specific title required for study in K–12 in Massachusetts by law.)

To understand, for example, *Federalist 10*, one of the most important writings in the debate to promote ratification of the Constitution, students must sustain full mental concentration over many dense (but not long) paragraphs. James Madison (Publius) coherently argues that liberty and faction (a special interest group) are essential in any healthy government system and that the best way to prevent the concentration of power in one or more special interest groups in a republican form of government is to encourage as many factions as possible so that no one faction can predominate.

What Madison expected of his readers then was common historical knowledge and some analogous experiences in local government. Readers today, especially young readers, need more. They clearly need a grasp of the vocabulary Madison used and some familiarity with the style he used to express his ideas. His long and complex sentences often contain qualifications of the ideas or generalizations he presents.

Probably the most difficult aspect of this *Federalist* paper (as well as others) for high school students is that Madison's writing is wholly at an abstract level of thinking. That is, he offers no names, places, events, and times as examples to ground the generalizations in almost every sentence.

There is no doubt that high school students today need some familiarity with the historical knowledge that Madison could expect his educated contemporaries to have. This knowledge includes an understanding of government in the ancient world and in several Italian city-states during the Renaissance, as well as ideas about self-government by Anglo-Scottish and French philosophers.

So, what are some possible texts that might be assigned in earlier grades in the English class, say from 6 to 10, to prepare students for reading *Federalist 10* in grade 11 or 12 with understanding? The sequence below demonstrates a curriculum development strategy called backmapping. In backmapping, one starts with an end goal or objective and works backwards (actually mostly forward), showing how one can get to that goal, grade by grade. In other words, one decides where one is going first, before plotting the journey to get there.

What Informational Texts or Literary Nonfiction Might Be Assigned in Grades 6 to 10

In grades 6 to 10, English or reading teachers could assign informational texts and literary nonfiction that address the Constitutional Convention, key figures attending it, the debate about the Constitution's innovative and/or controversial features, and the historical and philosophical background to the argument in *Federalist 10*. Each grade's readings should help students to accumulate gradually a body of information they can draw on when they first read *Federalist 10* (in conjunction with other related texts). For example:

For grades 6 and 7:

- Jean Fritz's *Alexander Hamilton: The Outsider* (judged to be readable in grades 4–6)
- Barbara Mitchell's *Father of the Constitution: A Story about James Madison* (RL 5.8)
- Letters between John and Abigail Adams

For grades 7, 8, and 9:

- Catherine Drinker Bowen's *Miracle at Philadelphia: The Story of the Constitutional Convention May-September 1787* (judged to be readable in grades 7–9)
- Jean Fritz's *Shh! We're Writing the Constitution* (RL 7.1)

For grades 9 and 10:

- *The Declaration of Independence*
- J. Hector St. John de Crèvecœur's *Letters from an American Farmer*

For grades 11 and 12:

- Marc M. Arkin's "'The Intractable Principle': David Hume, James Madison, Religion, and the Tenth Federalist," *American Journal of Legal History,* 1995, 39
- Montesquieu's *Spirit of the Laws* (written in 1748)
- James Madison's *Notes on the Constitutional Convention*
- Benjamin Franklin's *Autobiography* (RL 11.8)
- John Kaminski's *James Madison: Champion of Liberty and Justice*
- Garry Wills's *Explaining America: The Federalist*

What Imaginative Literary Texts Might Be Assigned in Grades 6 to 11?

English or reading teachers also need to assign some foundational works of American literature written in the eighteenth or nineteenth century that illustrate the style, syntax, and vocabulary of written texts of this time. The content of literary readings assigned before grade 11 or 12 does not have to relate to the content of *Federalist 10.* These readings may well illustrate related themes, topics, or concepts that are embedded in this country's founding political documents and these readings could be analyzed for these themes, topics, or concept, but this substantive link is not necessary. Given the intellectual goals of CCRS, the chief purpose for assigning foundational literary readings at each grade level is to help today's students to develop skill in understanding the vocabulary, syntax, and style of pre-twentieth century American writing.

Keep in mind that other imaginative and informational texts should be assigned at each grade level and can reflect other cultures, periods of time, and literary movements. What is listed below are simply examples of texts teachers can assign in middle and lower high school grades to prepare students for addressing an upper high school standard on foundational works in our political history—one major intellectual goal of the high school curriculum.

The texts listed below for grades 6 to 10 also prepare students for addressing the upper high school standard on foundational works in American literature, another intellectual goal of the high school curriculum. They are all well-known works in American literature.

But the goal is not just to familiarize students with them or their authors but to use them to develop skills for reading the basic political documents that inform their understanding of American principles, procedures, and institutions. How can students do well on tests requiring reading of primary sources written in the late eighteenth century when they have no general knowledge of the eighteenth century or familiarity with literary or other texts written in that time period?

For grades 6 and 7:

- Mark Twain's *Adventures of Tom Sawyer* (RL 8.1)
- Washington Irving's *Legend of Sleepy Hollow, Rip Van Winkle* (RL 11.1)

For grades 7, 8, and 9:

- Washington Irving's *Tales of the Alhambra, The Adventures of Captain Bonneville*
- James Fenimore Cooper's *Leatherstocking Tales*, especially *Last of the Mohicans* (RL 12.0)
- Frederick Douglass's *Narrative of the Life of Frederick Douglass an American Slave, Written by Himself* (RL 7.9)
- Edgar Allan Poe's "The Gold-Bug," "The Pit and the Pendulum," and other short stories (RL 7.4–8.8)

For grades 9 and 10:

- Herman Melville's Billy Budd (RL 10.6); "Bartleby the Scrivener"
- Harriet Beecher Stowe's' *Uncle Tom's Cabin* (RL 9.3)
- William Cullen Bryant's poems

For grades 11 and 12:

- Nathaniel Hawthorne's *Scarlet Letter* (RL 11.7)
- Herman Melville's *Moby-Dick* (RL 10.3)
- Mark Twain's *Adventures of Huckleberry Finn* (RL 6.6)

Summary

Common Core's grade-level reading standards do not suggest how to link works in order to build substantive civic and literary knowledge over the course of one grade or over several grades (i.e., they do not indicate basic principles for coherent curriculum sequences). But several standards at the upper high school level do provide substantive goals for the K–12 curriculum that most parents and other citizens would agree on.

Moreover, an appendix to the main document lists titles of literary and nonliterary works grouped by genre that illustrate a desirable range of reading difficulty in the upper high school grades (and at every grade level from K–12). As Common Core makes clear, they are exemplars of grade-level difficulty, not required readings for each grade. The purpose of this appendix is to underline the point that students should be reading successively more complex or difficult texts through the grades.

CONCLUDING REMARKS

Two Common Core standards in the high school years require the reading of several of this country's foundational documents. These two intellectually rich standards should be used as guides for selecting imaginative and informational texts in earlier grades to develop some of the content knowledge as well as the reading skills needed for civic literacy and authentic college-level coursework.

After selecting specific seminal documents in the Founding Period to teach in grades 11 and 12, English teachers and curriculum specialists also need to select other texts for grades 6 to 10 to ensure that students are progressively acquiring the knowledge and the familiarity with pre-twentieth American writing needed for reading these seminal documents. This is one way to create coherent curriculum sequences for both informational and imaginative texts over many grades.

Backmapping (setting forth an end goal at a higher grade level and then working toward it from earlier grade levels) can also be done with just the standard on foundational works of American literature. Here, too, works should be staged in increasing levels of reading difficulty so that students progressively acquire familiarity with the style of pre-twentieth century American writing.

IMPLICATIONS FOR PROFESSIONAL
DEVELOPMENT AND TEACHER LICENSURE

English teachers who teach high school students how to read and understand this country's seminal political documents ought to understand their historical context and philosophical background. Since English teachers probably majored in English, it is unlikely that they were required to study the context and background for these documents, as one would expect history and U.S. government majors to have done.

The lack of an academic background in political philosophy and history means that high school English teachers may need professional development in the context and background of the political documents their school boards or English departments have decided to require them to teach their students how to read, as well as those they also choose to teach. No one is better equipped to provide this professional development than departments of political science and political philosophy in their state's own colleges or universities.

It is reasonable to assume that most preparation programs for English teachers do not require prior coursework in political science and U.S. history. Thus, departments of political science and political philosophy in each state's colleges or universities should begin inquiries about what coursework should be required of aspiring English teachers or taken to satisfy core distribution requirements.

It may well be that prospective English teachers should be required to take coursework on the Constitutional Period from both U.S. history and political science faculty in their state's colleges or universities. Or perhaps prospective English teachers, in order to address Common Core's standards, should be taking interdisciplinary coursework involving collaborating faculty in the English, U.S. history, political science, and philosophy departments. Here are several recommendations for state departments of education to consider:

1. Require all U.S. government, history, and English teachers to participate once every five years in a We the People summer institute if they continue to be funded by Congress. These institutes are offered in almost every state every year by the Center for Civic Education in Calabasas, California. They are among the most academically rigorous workshops available for K–12 teachers and should be approved for

professional development credits as part of the required credits teachers must accumulate for license renewal.

2. Require accreditation of teacher preparation programs in U.S. history or U.S. government in a state's institutions of higher education by professional associations dedicated to the discipline of history or political science. If accreditation or program approval is to be carried out by the National Council for the Social Studies for the National Council for the Accreditation of Teacher Education, the state board of education or the state department of education can ask discipline-based organizations to provide peer reviewers for these programs.

3. Require demanding licensure tests in U.S. and world history and in U.S. government that stress the history of Western political thought and the Enlightenment. A good high school student could easily pass most existing teacher tests in history or social studies. At present, the major companies that construct teacher tests use professional peers—teachers and faculty in higher education (including schools of education)—for reviewing test items and determining cut scores. However, test items and passing scores for teacher tests are more likely to reflect fear that demanding tests will produce high failure rates (with political and economic consequences for the state's teacher preparation programs) than to reflect appropriate academic standards.

IMPLICATIONS FOR THE HIGH SCHOOL HISTORY/U.S. GOVERNMENT CURRICULUM

1. Require a U.S. government course to be given in the fall semester of grade 12 and to address Western political philosophy and the Founding Period in-depth. No student should graduate from an American high school without an upper high school-level understanding of such basic political principles as limited government, consent of the people, balance of powers, checks and balances, and an independent judiciary.

It would be desirable for high schools to standardize their course offerings so that all students take a U.S. government course in the fall of grade 12 and to arrange for their teachers to collaborate with English teachers when the required documents are being taught. It would also be helpful if the textbook used by U.S. government teachers facilitated study of these required documents.

2. Allow for and encourage *two consecutive years of U.S. history* in high school. The possibility of two consecutive years of U.S. history, whether in grades 9–10 or 10–11, was built into the 2003 Massachusetts History and Social Science Curriculum Framework, and many U.S. history teachers in Massachusetts told department of education staff that this was the best gift they could ever have been given, whether or not they liked the new standards. A two-year U.S. history course at the high school level would enable history teachers to spend sufficient time on the Constitutional Period. They would have a clear incentive to do so if the state required a civics or U.S. history test for graduation that emphasized the Constitutional Period.

NOTES

1. Common Core State Standards Initiative, 2010. http://corestandards.org/the-standards.

2. National Assessment of Education Progress, The Nation's Report Card: Civics 2006 (Washington DC: National Center for Education Statistics, 2007), http://nces.ed.gov/nationsreportcard/pubs/main2006/2007476.asp.

3. National Assessment of Educational Progress, The Nation's Report Card: Civics 2010 (Washington DC: National Center for Education Statistics. 2011), http://nces.ed.gov/pubsearch/pubsinfo.asp?pubid=2011466.

4. Circle Staff, "The Youth Vote in 2010: Final Estimates Based on Census Data," Circle Fact Sheet (Tufts University: Jonathan Tisch College for Citizenship and Public Service, 2011), 1.

5. Sandra Stotsky, "What Happens When History Teachers No Longer Understand the Founding?" *Academic Questions,* 2004, 17 (3): 21–51.

6. Mark Molli, staff member at the Center for Civic Education, e-mail message to author, May 17, 2011. Molli said: "Our research over the past three years indicates that 45 states require students to take a high school civics course. But questions exist about whether these requirements are enforced since many of these states do not require assessment linked to their graduation requirement."

7. John Patrick, professor emeritus of social studies at Indiana University, e-mail message to author, May 4, 2002.

8. David Conley, Understanding University Success, report from Standards for Success, a project of the Association of American Universities and the Pew Charitable Trusts, 2003, 23, section D.

9. http://www.act.org/news/pdf/study.pdf, p. 12.

10. http://www.corestandards.org/assets/CCSSI_ELA%20Standards.pdf.

9

Principles for Coherent Literature Sequences

By the twenty-first century, the official goals of the secondary literature curriculum in this country no longer include much literary and cultural knowledge. That is because forty-seven states by the end of 2011 have adopted Common Core's College and Career Readiness Standards for English Language Arts. As Chapter Seven noted, its College and Career Readiness Standards are content-free and culturally empty. However, as Chapter Eight discussed, some very important cultural knowledge is required in Common Core's high school grade-level standards.

It is not yet clear to what extent Common Core's few content-rich standards addressing this country's literature and foundational political documents will be assessed on the common tests at the high school level. Unlike the expectations built into, say, British Columbia's and Ireland's high school exit tests, it seems that U.S. students are no longer expected to be familiar with any particular literary text, author (except Shakespeare), or movement, although they are expected to be familiar with American literature of the eighteen, nineteenth, and early twentieth centuries.

Test items on the reading tests developed by the Programme for International Student Assessment (PISA) for fifteen-year-olds—tests favored by the U.S. Department of Education—reflect a completely culture-free skills-based approach. The unstated assumption is that no particular literary or nonliterary content knowledge could be common across the many countries and cultures participating in international tests.

Because of PISA's content-free objectives, it is quite possible that American high school students may increase their scores on future PISA reading tests despite a haphazard reading curriculum. Yet, without a coherent sequence of progressively more difficult readings, at least from grade 6 to grade 12, there is no reason to expect Critical Reading scores on the Scholastic Achievement Test (SAT) to increase rather than decrease, as they did from 2010 to 2011.

The purpose of this chapter is to present the principles that appear to undergird coherence in a literature curriculum, whether for one grade level and/or across several grade levels. It does so by showing the two coherent grade 6 curricula that served as the basis for abstracting these principles so that readers can judge for themselves whether they are indeed embedded in these curricula.

Historically, English teachers have used genres, literary elements, and literary techniques to organize the content of secondary literature curricula. They sometimes used the works of a significant author (e.g., Shakespeare) or the works of a particular region (e.g., Latin American literature) for a whole course. Historical periods and/or literary movements have almost always been used to organize year-long courses in American literature. Today teachers also use themes to organize titles as well as race, ethnicity, or gender. These are all organizing categories. But the principles that undergird a coherent sequence of literary works are not identical to them.

Different literature sequences in two very different programs for grade 6 help to explain the differences. While almost all of the books studied differ across these two programs, both sequences arrive at the same major title as the end-goal for the grade 6 literature curriculum. The reasons for the sequence in each school will be described before the principles that appear to underlie both curricula are spelled out.

A MULTI-YEAR LITERATURE SEQUENCE FOR GRADE 6 TO GRADE 8

The Brearley School is a highly regarded private school for academically strong girls in Manhattan.[1] Brearley's intellectually rigorous and coherent literature curriculum is the kind of curriculum that should be available in our public schools to a majority of students starting in grade 8 or 9. The amount of writing done and responded to by teachers in this particular private school may well reflect the low teacher-student ratios that high tuition makes possible, but the rationale for the titles assigned is independent of tuition costs.

Grade 6

- Folk Tales (summer reading continued into the fall): A large number are read and a few are selected for class discussion. They include: "The Valiant Chattee-Maker" (Indian), "The Young Head of the Family" (Chinese), and "The Wonderful Tar-Baby" (African-American).
- Ballads: Five Scottish ballads—"Sir Patrick Spens," "Edward, Edward," "Mary Hamilton," "The Twa Corbies," and "Barbra Allen," the last two having available English counterparts.
- *Book of Genesis*, King James Version, with some abridgement.
- Greek mythology, based on selections from Ovid's *Metamorphoses*, *The Iliad*, and *The Homeric Hymns*.
- *The Odyssey*

The grade 6 curriculum, like the curricula of other grades, is the product of the collective wisdom of many teachers over many years. All Brearley teachers teach at three or four different grade levels simultaneously. While such variety refreshes the teacher, it serves a more important purpose. It means that students receive instruction from teachers who know what their students will go on to learn and what they have already learned; texts read in one grade can be confidently referred to in another grade.

Cross-grade teaching also means that when the curriculum of a lower grade is revised, it is redesigned with the knowledge and skills in mind that older students must have or develop for reading the literary content of the higher grades. Overall, cross-grade teaching in the same year helps to maintain students' experience of a coherent curriculum.

The purpose of the grade 6 curriculum is to develop student understanding of major sources of allusion and reference in literature (broadly conceived) and major elements in literary texts (narrative structures, imagery, theme, irony, and style), and to ensure sufficient time for teaching students how to read closely. The last instructional goal explains why the grade 6 curriculum begins with the folk tale unit and occupies just under two weeks.

The tales chosen have strong plots as well as characters whose words and deeds clearly reveal their traits. Their syntax is simple, allowing teachers to direct attention to what is beneath the surface—to close reading. These tales let teachers address literary elements such as narrative structure, imagery, theme, irony, and style. These concepts are new to sixth graders.

The unit on Scottish ballads, which students must read aloud, legitimizes so-called "misspellings," as in the opening to "Sir Patrick Spens":

The king sits in Dumferling toune,
Drinking the blude-reid wine,
"O whar sall I get guid sailor,
To sail this schip of mine?"

Students enjoy pronouncing the Scottish "r" and the now-silent "k" and guttural "gh" in "knight." More important, since words need to be looked at very closely in the pronunciation of such sounds and often analogized to make their meaning clear, reading ballads aloud forces student to pay close attention to each word and phrase, such attention being precisely the skill they will need when they begin to look at more sophisticated literary texts.

The ballads themselves are highly dramatic—full of murder and betrayal—and highly elliptical, with plot elements that must be inferred. Such reading material turns students into little Inspector Clouseaus, training them to read between the lines, to make inferences from the evidence before them—what was the "counseil" given Edward by his "mither"?—who murdered the "new-slain knight"?—and to find corroborative evidence within the rest of the ballad for whatever conclusions they reach. Comparing two versions of the same ballad provides additional experience in close reading.

Students then read a somewhat abridged version of the King James *Book of Genesis*, taught as a narrative rather than as a religious text. Its stories, too, are elliptical and require precisely the same close attention that the ballad unit has demanded. There are, additionally, vocabulary words, complex character studies, aspects of style, and recurring motifs, among other features. Because students will go on to read some of the most culturally and/or historically significant works of English and American literature in higher grades, many of which allude to the language, stories, and concepts in Genesis, this one unit alone equips them to read future works with fuller understanding and therefore with greater pleasure.

The other major source of allusion and reference in the literature students will read in higher grades comes from classical mythology, and so they study Greek mythology for the next six or seven weeks. Different teachers approach this unit in different ways. Some approach the study of mythology through selections from Ovid's *Metamorphoses*. Others use excerpts from *The Iliad* and *The Homeric Hymns*. The mythology unit, like the rest of the grade 6 curriculum, is taught using primary, not secondary, literary sources.

The curriculum for grade 6 ends with *The Odyssey*, which is read in its entirety in the Rieu prose translation. In many schools, public and private, *The Odyssey* is taught in grade 9 or in grade 11, as at Hunter College High School. The only difference between teaching it to younger or older students is the pace at which students can proceed. A sixth grader at Brearley can read about fifteen pages a night (one *Odyssey* chapter or "Book"), and with three assigned nights per week—and a number of writing assignments—*The Odyssey* unit occupies about eleven to twelve weeks.

A school whose students are literate by grade 6 and whose homes reflect a high level of literacy can begin serious learning earlier than might otherwise be the case. Its grade 6 curriculum makes it possible for teachers in grades 7 and 8 to make substantive connections with what they know students have already read and with concepts that they know students have already absorbed. The approach to the material is not thematic; rather, teachers focus on whatever is particularly notable about each work.

Grade 7

- *Haroun and the Sea of Stories*, RL 6.9 (summer reading)
- Poetry: Browning's "My Last Duchess," Shelley's "Ozymandias," Blake's "The Poison Tree," Bishop's "The Filling Station," Toomer's "Reapers," and others
- *Great Expectations*, RL 9.2
- *Julius Caesar*, RL 10.8

Grade 7 begins with a poetry unit and introduces students to a set of literary terms to learn and apply. As in grade 6, the purpose for placing short works of literature at the beginning of the school year is to control the proportion of reading to analysis in order to ensure an instructional emphasis on close reading.

In contrast, the two works that follow, *Great Expectations* and *Julius Caesar*, are very long and require sustained focus. *Great Expectations* also ramps up the amount of reading time for students each evening and leads to training in selective note-taking for each chapter. While very challenging to young students, the text is emotionally accessible.

Grade 8

- *Jane Eyre*, RL 7.9 (summer reading assignment)
- Short Stories (studied in depth): Galsworthy's "The Japanese Quince," Poe's "The Cask of Amontillado," Hawthorne's "Young Goodman Brown," Joyce's "Araby," Baldwin's "The Rockpile"; other short stories read: Lawrence's "The Rocking-Horse Winner," Joyce's "Eveline," Cheever's "The Swimmer," Walker's "Everyday Use," Mansfield's "Miss Brill," Murakami's "The Town of Cats," and others. (Three of these stories are discussed briefly, anticipatory to students selecting and writing analytically about one of them.)
- Poetry of many periods and types, the criteria being whether the poems are understandable in emotional and intellectual terms to students of this age: Poems are by Coleridge, Frost, Hardy, Hayden, Heaney, Hopkins, Wordsworth, Shakespeare, and others.
- *Frankenstein*, RL 12.4
- *Twelfth Night*, RL 8.6, or *A Midsummer Night's Dream*, RL, 10.9

Grade 8 begins with *Jane Eyre*, the text assigned as summer reading, and then moves quickly to an extended short story unit. The short story unit functions in grade 8 in much the way that the poetry unit functions in grade 7 and the folk tales in grade 6—to ensure an instructional emphasis on close reading.

This unit includes the teaching of basic narrative terminology and components and close examination of the way such components as plot, character, setting, theme, irony, and imagery appear in the different short stories. Plot structure and theme emerge more easily when students deal with short works, and the large number of short works that can be assigned allows students to experience the analytical process over and over again.

The second portion of the short story unit consists of a long (four- to five-page) analytical essay on an additional story. At no time, in grade 7 or grade 8—or elsewhere in the English curriculum—does an analytical exercise refer to or draw on anything but a primary source text. Students in grade 8 then read *Frankenstein* and *Twelfth Night* or *A Midsummer Night's Dream,* both of which seem easier to them than *Great Expectations* and *Julius Caesar* despite the complexity of these works. As with *Julius Caesar, Twelfth Night* or *A Midsummer Night's Dream* is read aloud almost in its entirety in class and examined closely.

The Brearley curriculum may contain fewer texts than the curriculum of some other schools because much time is spent in close examination of most of the texts read. Nevertheless, throughout the secondary curriculum an attempt is made to include examples from all major literary types (poetry, drama, fiction) each year.

AN INTENSIVE FOURTEEN-MONTH LITERATURE SEQUENCE BEGINNING IN GRADE 6

The series of titles listed below (and their readability levels using ATOS for Books) is taught in the Rainier Scholars program, a private program in Seattle beginning in grade 6 that recruits students chiefly from the Seattle public schools. The program, begun in 2002, is for "African American, Hispanic Latino, Native American, and first generation Asian American students" who "demonstrate a strong work ethic and motivation combined with the cognitive ability to thrive in college prep settings."

About sixty students in grade 5 are selected each year for the grade 6 program. They have agreed to spend two summers doing intensive academic work, take after-school classes every Wednesday and Saturday for the entire school year, and do three hours of homework every night. The primary purpose of the fourteen-month program is to prepare the students for and to place them in demanding academic programs at higher grade levels, in public or private schools.[2] The program also gives students individual mentoring, tutoring, and counseling from the end of grade 5 through college.

The larger goal for the grade 6 curriculum is moral development, and discussion of the books in each unit is guided by one or two prepared questions relating to moral development, which differ across units (e.g., for the first unit, the question is: "How do we decide right from wrong?" for the fourth unit, the question is: "How do people fight with integrity?" and for *The Odyssey* the question is: "What makes a good leader?"). According to the literature specialist for this program, all students must read all these books, which increase in reading difficulty, overall, from the first two units to the final two. The grouping of the books in each unit was guided in part by R. S. Crane's typology for plots: plots of action, plots of character, and plots of thought.[3]

The first Unit

- Jerry Spinelli's *Milkweed*, RL 3.6;
- Lloyd Alexander's *Westmark*, RL 5.3; and
- Harper Lee's *To Kill a Mockingbird*, RL 5.6.

The second unit

- Kate DiCamillo's *Tale of Despereaux*, RL 4.7;
- Jacqueline Woodsons' Maizon at Blue Hill, RL 4.1;
- Jennifer Donnelly's *A Northern Light*, RL 4.5; and
- Richard Wright's *Black Boy*, RL 7.4.

The third unit

- Salman Rushdie's *Haroun and the Sea of Stories*, RL 6.9;
- Ingri d'Aulaire's *Greek Myths*, RL 6.6;
- Ingri d'Aulaire's *Norse Myths*;
- Richard Chase's "Jack in the Giant's New Ground" from *The Jack Tales*, RL 4.8;
- Richard Chase's "Jack and the Bean Tree" from *The Jack Tales*, RL 4.8; and
- Kate DiCamillo's *The Miraculous Journey of Edward Tulane*, RL 4.4.

The fourth unit

- Ellen Levine's *Freedom's Children*, RL 6.3;
- John Steinbeck's *The Pearl*, RL 7.1;

- Reginald Rose's *Twelve Angry Men*; and
- Rosemary Sutcliff's *Black Ships Before Troy*, RL 6.8.

The fifth unit

- Shakespeare's *Romeo and Juliet*, RL 8.6.

The sixth unit

- Homer's *The Odyssey*, RL 10.3.

The guiding questions for each unit also serve to unify the two different sets of ideas connecting the books within and across units to help
provide coherence to the sequence. One set of ideas is the undertaking
of a fantasy adventure by recognizable human beings or personified animals (e.g., *Westmark, Tale of Despereaux*, and *The Miraculous Journey
of Edward Tulane*).

The danger-laden journeys that develop or challenge the protagonist's
character blend first into adventure tales with magical backgrounds (*The
Jack Tales* and *Haroun and the Sea of Stories*) and then into the fantasy
adventures of supernatural beings, human beings with superhuman qualities, and phantasmagorical creatures in the classical myths that have supplied the imagery, metaphors, and characters for succeeding generations
of writers. These texts prepare students for Sutcliff's rendition of *The
Iliad* in her novel *Black Ships Before Troy*. This work, in turn, eases students into the culminating work, *The Odyssey*, the work with the highest
reading level in the fourteen-month sequence.

Another set of connecting ideas relates to the moral questions raised by
prejudice and the hostility or violence it may provoke in the real world.
The chosen books show that unacceptable behavior by some people has
been directed against other people not only on the basis of racial or ethnic
stereotypes in this country (e.g., *To Kill a Mockingbird, Maizon at Blue
Hill, Black Boy, Freedom's Children,* and *Twelve Angry Men*) but also
on the basis of common or commonly perceived characteristics relating
to ethnic and/or cultural differences in other countries as well (*Milkweed,
The Pearl*) and idiosyncratic family relationships in the same society
(*Romeo and Juliet*).

PRINCIPLES FOR DEVELOPING
COHERENCE AND CRITICAL THINKING

Although the final selection in grade 6 in both school programs is the same, the curricula leading to *The Odyssey* differ. A few units studied earlier in the school year (on Greek myths) were similar, but entirely different titles were used to prepare students for the final selection: Ingri d'Aulaire's *Greek Myths* in the Seattle program, and Ovid's *Metamorphoses*, *The Iliad*, and *The Homeric Hymns* at the Brearley School. Genre and literary characteristics seem to be the major focus of the staging process in one school, while questions about content and the structural features associated with a life-changing epic voyage tend to dominate the staging process in the other school.

At least four common principles appear to underlie the literature sequences for grade 6 in both the Brearley and the Rainier Scholars program.

(1) Texts read in the early part of the school year or in earlier grades have substantive links to texts read later in the school year and/or in later grades. This principle reflects in part the basic tenets of schema theory, or the idea that we organize information in ways that facilitate memorization and retention. Pedagogy based on this theory seeks to help students to develop connections among ideas for understanding and retaining new material.

(2) Assigned texts increase in reading difficulty over the course of one or several school years to develop students' cognitive capacity to handle more advanced vocabulary and complex sentence structure. This principle reflects the findings of one hundred years of research on the major sources of reading difficulty across a variety of texts.[4]

(3) Students study culturally and historically important literary and nonliterary works that stimulated the imagination or thoughts of later writers and continue to influence the language and literature students encounter as educated readers and writers of English. This principle reflects research in cognitive psychology on the knowledge base underlying reading comprehension and critical thinking.[5] Selection of curriculum content thus entails both discipline-based knowledge and professional judgment.

(4) Access to historically and culturally important literary texts is staged over the course of a grade level and across grade levels because these texts are usually difficult to read. This principle reflects teaching

experience, pedagogical judgments about sequencing, and research on such psychological constructs as "scaffolding."[6]

USE OF NONFICTION TO PROVIDE THE HISTORICAL AND CULTURAL CONTEXT FOR LITERARY READINGS

As historically organized courses in American and British literature usually demonstrate, chronology expressed through historical and literary periodization across centuries in a year-long high school course can help students to see how later writers were influenced (positively or negatively) by earlier writers. Periodization helps students to see links between imaginative and informational texts written at about the same time. A major work of nonfiction can also serve as the backbone of an English course to provide the historical and cultural context for a variety of imaginative texts. Here are several possibilities.

The first example is the *Harvard Encyclopedia of American Ethnic Groups* by Stephan Thernstrom, first published in 1980. Selections from this encyclopedia can effectively integrate short stories by members of this country's many ethnic and racial groups because it is a guide to the history, culture, and distinctive characteristics of the more than one hundred ethnic groups who live in the United States. It addresses not only the immigrants and refugees who came voluntarily but also those already in the New World when the first Europeans arrived, those whose ancestors came involuntarily as slaves, and those who became part of the American population as a result of conquest or purchase and subsequent annexation.

According to a description of the *Encyclopedia*, while the group entries are the heart of the book, it contains, in addition, a series of thematic essays illuminating key facets of ethnicity. Some of these are comparative; some philosophical; some historical; others focus on current policy issues or relate ethnicity to major subjects such as education, religion, and literature. American identity and Americanization, immigration policy and experience, and prejudice and discrimination in U.S. history are discussed at length. Several essays probe the complex interplay between assimilation and pluralism—perhaps the central theme in American history—and the complications of race and religion.

Selected encyclopedia entries together with short stories by immigrants from the selected groups can usefully complement a U.S. history course in grade 11 or 12. An article in the *English Journal* in 1994 titled "Academic Guidelines for Selecting Multiethnic and Multicultural Literature" provides a long list of recognized works by members of dozens of immigrant groups to this country in the nineteenth and twentieth centuries.[7]

Two more examples show how nonfiction texts can introduce grades 10–12 students to historically significant ideas and/or events, as well as provide the context for recognized literary texts linkable to the nonfiction text. One exemplar text centers on one of the most powerful ideas of the nineteenth and twentieth centuries: communism.

Leading intellectuals around the world chose to serve as supporters of the Soviet Union if not as members of the Communist Party itself. One of the interesting works to come out of the reflections of disaffected fellow-travelers was *The God That Failed*, a collection of essays by literary writers solicited and edited by Richard Crossman, British author and Labor Party politician, and published in 1949. The six essayist-contributors were Louis Fischer, André Gide, Arthur Koestler, Ignazio Silone, Stephen Spender, and Richard Wright. Their literary works include Koestler's *Darkness at Noon* (1940) and *The Yogi and the Commissar* (1945), Gide's *The Counterfeiters* (1926), Fischer's *The Life of Mahatma Gandhi* (1950) and *The Life of Lenin* (1964); Richard Wright's *Native Son* (1940) and *Black Boy* (1945), Silone's *Fontamara* (1934) and *Bread and Wine* (1936/1955), and Stephen Spender's *Poems* (1933).

As can be seen, the literary works of the essayists in Crossman's collection include biographies and poems. Most of the novels mentioned are relatively short. A curriculum that focuses on several essay writers in Crossman's volume together with one of their works (or a substantial excerpt) makes for a coherent and appropriately challenging semester-long or year-long course for high school students also taking a world history course. It clearly introduces them to the world of ideas and their consequences.

The other example draws on the work of Barbara Tuchman, a distinguished historian. *The Proud Tower: A Portrait of the World Before the War, 1890–1914* (1966) has chapters that can provide the background for such late nineteenth and early twentieth century titles as Emile Zola's "J'Accuse," Arthur Schnitzler's "La Ronde," Franz Kafka's "Metamorphosis," Anton Chekhov's *The Cherry Orchard*, and Thomas Mann's "Death in Venice."

High school students do not read any whole works of historical nonfiction today, as Will Fitzhugh of *The Concord Review* often notes, and Tuchman's work is an excellent introduction to well-written historical writing and to a period that receives inadequate attention in world history courses. This particular work focuses on the antecedents to World War I, the watershed event sparked by the assassination of Archduke Franz Ferdinand of Austria-Hungary by a young Serbian anarchist.

What happened during and after World War I helped to shape the rest of the twentieth century. Since Common Core's English language arts standards require all students to read far more nonfiction than ever before, the use of a critically acclaimed, well-written work of historical nonfiction about this period by a highly regarded historian would enhance students' knowledge base (and reading skills) in both their history and English courses.

The educational benefits of using a highly regarded work of nonfiction to provide the historical and cultural context for a group of imaginative texts in a year-long English course suggest a fifth principle. *The nonfiction taught in a year-long English course should provide the historical and cultural context for at least some of the imaginative literature also taught in that course.*

In other words, there should be something linking the major texts studied to establish coherence other than a proposed thematic relationship that may distort the meaning of the literary texts, or a simple topical relationship. And it would be far more educational to the teacher as well as the student if a well regarded and authentic academic source provided the context for a literary work rather than the pedagogical apparatus supplied by an educational publisher.

CONCLUDING REMARKS

The purpose for a coherent curriculum in any subject is to help students to understand and retain the knowledge and skills needed for undertaking more difficult or complex academic work in that subject and in other related subjects. The five principles discussed in this chapter are not categories for organizing what is in the curriculum, such as genres or literary elements. Rather, they serve to guide the choice of categories for organizing texts or to monitor their placement.

As the grade 6 curricula in the Rainier Scholars program and the Brearley School suggest, academic expectations for the diversity of able students in this country can be similar. This principle is based on the social and political concept of equity. Both programs appear to share the belief that when given a coherent and challenging curriculum, able grade 6 students, regardless of gender and racial background, can rise to that challenge. These programs imply that what is beneficial to able students in grade 6 should also be made available to other students in higher grades in our public schools.

POINTS TO REMEMBER

(1) Texts read in the early part of the school year or in earlier grades should have substantive links to texts read later in the school year and/or in later grades.

(2) Assigned texts should increase in reading difficulty over the course of a school year or several school years to develop students' cognitive capacity to handle more advanced vocabulary and complex sentence structure (among other features of these texts).

(3) Students should study culturally and historically important works that stimulated the imagination or thoughts of later writers and that continue to influence the language that students listen to, read, and write.

(4) Access to historically and culturally important literary texts should be staged over the course of a grade level and across grade levels because these texts are usually difficult to read.

(5) The nonfiction taught in a year-long English course should provide the historical and cultural context for at least some of the imaginative literature taught in that course.

NOTES

1. Most of the information on the Brearley curriculum comes from the school's website. It was supplemented by Helaine Smith, an English teacher at the school.

2. The information on the Rainier Scholars program comes from what is posted on the Internet. The literature specialist for the program, Drego Little, sent me a copy of the grade 6 curriculum and confirmed my analysis of it.

3. See, for example, R. S. Crane, "The Concept of Plot and the Plot of 'Tom Jones,'" in *Critics and Criticism: Ancient and Modern*, ed. R. S. Crane (Chicago: University of Chicago Press, 1952).

4. The results of the one hundred-year-old body of research on readability, leading to the development of a variety of readability formulas, are in essence a conclusion that some measure of vocabulary load and some measure of syntactic complexity (sentence structure) are the major components of readability. There are other features of a text that can predict reading difficulty to some extent (e.g., paragraph density) but none as well as these two basic features. See also Appendix A in the "Common Core State Standards for English Language Arts and Literacy in History/Social Science, Science, and Technical Subjects," 2010.

5. See Dan Willingham, *Why Don't Students Like School? A Cognitive Scientist Answers Questions About How the Mind Works and What It Means for the Classroom* (New York: Jossey Bass, 2009) for a review of the relevant research.

6. This concept comes from the work of Lev Vygotsky, a Soviet psychologist (1896–1934). Vygotsky stated that a child follows an adult's example and gradually develops the ability to do certain tasks without help. Vygotsky's definition of the zone of proximal development presents it as the distance between a child's actual developmental level as determined by independent problem solving and the level of potential development as determined through problem solving under adult guidance, or in collaboration with more capable peers (L. S. Vygotsky, *Mind in Society: The Development of Higher Psychological Processes*, eds. M. Cole, V. John-Steiner, S. Scribner, & E. Souberman (Cambridge, MA: Harvard University Press, 1978), 86.

7. Sandra Stotsky, "Academic Guidelines for Selecting Multiethnic and Multicultural Literature," *English Journal*, 1994, 83 (2): 27–34.

Doing the "Right Thing": Comedy and Political Satire in Grade 8

Jamie Highfill

To be culturally literate is to possess the basic information needed to thrive in the modern world. The breadth of that information is great, extending over the major domains of human activity from sports to science. It is by no means confined to "culture" narrowly understood as an acquaintance with the arts. Nor is it confined to one social class. Quite the contrary. Cultural literacy constitutes the only sure avenue of opportunity for disadvantaged children, the only reliable way of combating the social determinism that now condemns them to remain in the same social and educational condition as their parents. That children from poor and illiterate homes tend to remain poor and illiterate is an unacceptable failure of our schools, one which has occurred not because our teachers are inept but chiefly because they are compelled to teach a fragmented curriculum based on faulty educational theories.[1]

—E. D. Hirsch

It is widely accepted that schools across America are failing our children, and teachers as easy scapegoats are consistently blamed for students' mediocre achievement. Arkansas's schools are no exception. Arkansas, like many other states, does not have a set curriculum for each grade level. Rather, it has standards that are touted as a curriculum. In fact, the standards in the English language arts are language arts skill sets posing as a curriculum in something called a curriculum framework. This essay describes the literature curriculum I developed for grade 8 students to address the substantive gaps in the fragmented curriculum they had experienced.

THE SKILLS-BASED CURRICULUM IN ARKANSAS

The use of language arts skill sets as the curriculum is a tenet of educational formalism, which E. D. Hirsch describes as "the . . . principle that specific information is irrelevant to 'language arts skills.'"[2] He goes on to explain: "Educational formalism holds that reading and writing are like baseball and skating; formalism conceives of literacy as a set of techniques that can be developed by proper coaching and practice."[3] While students are learning to read, practicing skills makes sense. But once students start reading to learn (usually by grade 3 or 4) and practicing those skills on texts that increase in difficulty with each grade level, the baseball analogy Hirsch talks about changes the game.

Arkansas students don't know how to swing at any text because its own standards do not delineate particular texts (or choices of texts) on which to practice those skills. And because Arkansas's standards are devoid of guidelines to specific *content* on which students might practice their "language arts skills," there is usually little coherence in the group of texts teachers choose for any grade level, and no coherent sequencing across grade levels. As a result, from each grade level students bring myriad kinds of background knowledge to the educational party at the next grade level. Hirsch said it well in *The Knowledge Deficit* when he defended teachers:

> so-called low teacher quality is not an innate characteristic of American teachers; it is the consequence of the training they have received and of the vague, incoherent curricula they are given to teach, both of which result from an ed school de-emphasis on specific, cumulative content. No teacher, however capable, can efficiently cope with the huge differences in academic preparation among the students in a typical American classroom—differences that grow with each successive grade.[4]

Nevertheless, Arkansas teachers have been expected to create specific classroom curricula based on Arkansas's "standards," or skill sets, which amounts to creating something out of nothing. They have therefore become territorial about what they're teaching, which manifests itself to an outsider as resistance to change or to new ideas. It isn't. Because these teachers have invested so much time and energy hacking a path through the jungle of content choices to teach to these standards, their burden has been unnecessarily increased and, as a result, they are tired. The thought of having to go through that process again is exhausting.

Is it any wonder why there are jokes about teachers who laminate their lesson plans? Who would want to constantly create and recreate something out of nothing? And how can teachers be the "keepers of knowledge" if they don't know what knowledge they're supposed to keep?

About ten years ago the Fayetteville Public Schools attempted to align courses of study in each subject both horizontally and vertically by having teachers meet in content-specific groups for one or two days each year to plan and sequence. At first, vertical subject area teams included teachers who taught Pre-Advanced Placement (Pre-AP) and Advanced Placement (AP) courses in the subject, but those groups were disbanded over five years ago. The process had turned territorial and little progress was made.

Frustrated teachers ended up going back to their classrooms and doing what they had always done, saying "this too shall pass." Increasing their frustration were questions from new teachers like: "What texts do I teach?" and "How do I know where to start with my students if I don't know what they've read?" When terms like "intellectual property" were bandied about, how would anyone know what he or she could use and what was "hands off?"

Students have regularly come to grade 8 English each year with scattered background knowledge. When I was a new teacher, I too didn't know where to start. Some students had not read Robert Frost in grade 7; others had never heard of Tom Sawyer; and one student referred to Benjamin Franklin as "the kite guy." When I expressed horror that students could not come up with any other information about one of this country's founders other than that he was "the kite guy," an administrator said: "At least he knew that."

What can be done about the bigger issue at stake here—that students do not have a firm cultural foundation upon which to build the rest of their education? No wonder that curricula continue to be revised and dumbed down in an attempt to find a common place from which to start. What is also ironic in this age of No Child Left Behind is that each year more and more students indicate that they do not understand widely used historical references and literary allusions on television, in books, and in films and, what is worse, do not even *know* that there are cultural and historical references in "texts" that deepen their meaning.

Many teachers hoped that the Common Core "curriculum" adopted by Arkansas in 2010 would assuage their anxieties about having to create something out of thin air again, to "fill" some of those "holes" in our students' educations. Most school districts created task forces to analyze the Common Core Standards and have held many meetings. A lot of energy has gone into the process of analysis, but the Fayetteville school district still does not have a real K–12 curriculum sequence fleshed out.

Anxiety is again up, and the age-old "resistance" is rearing its ugly head because information is being "doled" out to the faculty in small pieces without an overview of the big picture. "What is it going to look like?" is the question that keeps coming up. It's a good question because the new standards are also mostly skill sets, without direction to a coherent curriculum in which to practice the skills.

Hirsch said that "[p]reschool is not too early for starting earnest instruction in literate national culture. Fifth grade is almost too late. Tenth grade usually *is* too late."[5] And he's right. My grade 8 students will soon be in high school, and I can only begin to fill some of the holes in their background knowledge. The huge diversity of educational experiences most students have had makes it easy to understand why many teachers who love the subject they majored in and teach do not stay in the profession. Their task is overwhelming.

BACKGROUND TO A COHERENT
GRADE 8 LITERATURE CURRICULUM

I was hired to teach at Woodland Junior High School in Fall 2002 with funding from a Classroom Size Reduction Grant that had been awarded to the school district. I began in the middle of November, after the school had pulled students from the other grade 8 English classes to make up my class. The chair of the department sent the lesson plans she had taught since the beginning of the school year so that I could see what the students had already been exposed to. I was expected to develop my own curriculum for the rest of the school year.

Like all new teachers, I struggled to find ways to build a community of readers and writers and made my share of mistakes. But over the course of almost ten years, my classroom literature curriculum developed chiefly to fill in the missing pieces I perceived in my students' background knowledge. I teach what I believe will be essential to my students' success not only in high school Pre-AP and AP courses and any post-secondary educational institution they enroll in but also in assimilating into the civic culture in which they will live.

To start to lay some foundational knowledge for my students, I borrowed ideas from colleagues in the Northwest Arkansas Writing project, incorporated reading strategies from the Smart Step Literacy Lab Classroom project at Harding University, selected texts from reading lists for college-intending students, and drew on a copy of the Core Knowledge Sequence to identify grade appropriateness. I would have liked to collaborate with departmental colleagues, but most of them did not indicate a consistent interest in planning together. Therefore, I forged my calendar and my literature curriculum alone.

One of the big gaps in students' background knowledge related to understanding political satire and comedy in literature. My perception of this gap arose from the effort to help young students understand the cultural references behind cartoons. Other kinds of humorous texts soon came to mind, especially "The Secret Life of Walter Mitty," also an excellent text with which to teach close reading because his character is revealed through detailed analysis of his "jargon." T. S. Eliot is quoted as saying about James Thurber's work:

It is a form of humor which is also a way of saying something. There is a criticism of life at the bottom of it. It is serious and even somber. Unlike so much of humor, it is not merely a criticism of manners—that is, of the superficial aspects of society at a given moment—but something more profound.[6]

The elements of comedy in literature thus became one focus in my classroom curriculum.

Enjoyment of political satire in particular demands a great deal of cultural knowledge, and social and political humor extending from self-deprecatory remarks to biting satire is a striking characteristic of American and British writing. Few literary traditions have had so many authors so merciless about the political foibles of their own society (and other societies). George Orwell's *Animal Farm* thus became the major novel for study in my curriculum. Moreover, it is not difficult to read, it has only ten chapters, and its political allusions are easy to understand because my grade 8 students spend a great deal of time in social studies classes learning about types of governments. It is also rich with symbolism and allusions to other ideas and character types, so it can be linked to many other pieces of literature over the course of the year.

Beast fables/epics, fairy tales, fables, allegories, and parables were then included so that students could understand genres that were intended for didactic purposes, reflect on Orwell's choice of genre for his political satire, and learn how to connect what educators call "big ideas" across texts. For example, the perversion of the notion of equality in *Animal Farm* could help students understand its perversion in Kurt Vonnegut's short story "Harrison Bergeron."

Students also had no basic knowledge of Arthurian legends or quest literature, so they did not understand chivalry, what a hero is, words like "quixotic," or such phrases as "tilting at windmills." It became *my* quest to teach students where the meanings of common ideas, words, and allusions in our culture come from.

Finally, students had not learned to do close reading. Even though most had read "The Tell-Tale Heart" in grade 7, they didn't know the significance of the title or that the old man had simply had a heart attack.

Carol Jago, past president of the National Council of Teachers of English, once said at a seminar that the "teaching of language is the teaching of what it means to be human." What it means to be human in our culture became the long-term goal of my curriculum.

To repeat, my classroom literature curriculum was developed as a response to perceived gaps in my grade 8 students' background knowledge and as bridges to texts they may encounter in later years. Compatibility with Common Core's "standards" was unintentional, as most of the texts in my curriculum were chosen prior to Arkansas's adoption of those standards in 2010. And because Common Core only *suggests* titles as examples of complexity and its "standards" are as skills-based as Arkansas's own standards were, my curriculum is as valid as any others that may be perceived to align with Common Core's standards.

MY GRADE 8 LITERATURE CURRICULUM

The only way to teach kids to read texts for meaning is to give them lots and lots of meaningful texts to read. Henry David Thoreau said: "Read the best books first, or you may not have a chance to read them at all."[7] Therefore, the chosen texts include but are not limited to:

- Short stories by Edgar Allan Poe, James Thurber, Kurt Vonnegut, O. Henry, and Neil Gaiman
- Fairy tales by the Brothers Grimm, Roald Dahl, and Hans Christian Andersen
- Beast epics, beast fables, and pourquoi stories by Rudyard Kipling, Joel Chandler Harris, and Aesop
- Allegories or parables: *Everyman*, Plato's "The Allegory of the Cave"
- Poems by Robert Frost, Dylan Thomas, Walt Whitman, Emily Dickinson, Robert Herrick, Lewis Carroll, William Shakespeare, Elizabeth Barrett Browning, Matthew Arnold, Leigh Hunt, May Riley Smith, Lord Byron, and Rudyard Kipling
- Films and excerpts that complement literature study: *Bang, Bang, You're Dead; The Princess Bride; Excalibur; Man of La Mancha; Harold and Maude; Shakespeare in Love; Can't Buy Me Love*
- *Animal Farm*, portions of *I Know Why the Caged Bird Sings*
- Speeches: "I Have a Dream," John F. Kennedy's Inaugural Address, and Polonius's speech from *Hamlet*

Several children's poems are included as "access" pieces and for teaching figurative language. I drew from Shel Silverstein's *A Light in the Attic* and *Where the Sidewalk Ends*, Judith Viorst's *If I Were in Charge of the World* and *Other Worries: Poems for Children and their Parents*, and Dr. Seuss's books for concepts such as alliteration, assonance, consonance, simile, metaphor, and onomatopoeia. I incorporated popular music (e.g., by

Cat Stevens, Blue Oyster Cult, Coolio, Weird Al Yankovic, the Righteous Brothers, the Police, and Billy Joel) to teach annotation; concepts such as tone, theme, parody, and mood; ideas such as quest, growing up, identity, independence, and obsession; and compare/contrast strategies.

I provide students with their own copies of all the texts we read so they can mark them up and practice highlighting. All copies are taped and/or stapled into their notebooks.

HOW THIS CURRICULUM IS TAUGHT

The first two weeks of school are spent building a reading and writing community in the classroom. Literature study begins in the third week with the analysis of character development in the 2002 film *Bang, Bang, You're Dead* since characters are the easiest way for many students to access literature. While watching the film, students take notes on who the character is, how he acts, how others react to him, and how stereotypes about who "good kids" and "bad kids" are shape our perceptions. I point out allusions they do not recognize and we discuss how those allusions add layers of meaning for the "reader." Music from the film is included in their analysis, that is, how it contributes to character development.

Short stories are then used to teach other major elements of literature: setting, dialogue, plot, and theme. Students discuss setting in "The Tell-Tale Heart," internal dialogue and jargon in "The Secret Life of Walter Mitty," and plot structure in "The Gift of the Magi." Students are encouraged to make inferences about such ideas as obsession and fear, ageism, stereotypes and prejudice, rebellion, and selflessness and to infer a theme for each story. I continue to note and discuss allusions.

At this point I introduce a close reading strategy called T-W-I-S-T (T-tone; W-word choice and diction; I-imagery and detail; S-style; and T-theme) to aid students in learning what to look for when they annotate their texts. Some poetry is also incorporated with the study of short stories when poems have titles that seem to coincide with the ideas in the stories. Students must make their own connections between the stories and the poems.

After the short story unit, students begin their study of *Animal Farm* looking first at characterization, setting, dialogue, and plot. They then learn about symbolism and metaphorical allusions in characters' names and actions, willing suspension of disbelief, rhetorical questions and devices, satire and irony, and propaganda and bias in dialogue. They extract Orwell's ideas about fear, ageism, oppression, rebellion, and anarchy as well as freedom, conscience, and responsibility.

They also analyze Vonnegut's story "Harrison Bergeron" for satire, irony, and oxymorons (as well as for its ideas about anarchy, rebellion, misguided egalitarianism, and jealousy), and make comparisons with those elements in *Animal Farm*. They look at these elements in beast epics, beast fables, allegories, parables, fables, and fairy tales as well.

To understand better the "why" of Orwell's decision to use a genre traditionally associated with children, they analyze tricksters, anthropomorphism, and didactics in Aesop's fables and the Anansi stories. Selections from Kipling's *Just So Stories* reinforce students' background knowledge about character types and also provide other examples of didacticism.

Selections from *I Know Why The Caged Bird Sings* are used for comparison with the style of the oral tradition in Joel Chandler Harris's "The Wonderful Tar Baby" and "How Mr. Rabbit Was Too Sharp for Mr. Fox" and to complement the expression of oppression and fear in Orwell's novel. Since Maya Angelou is from Arkansas, her story strikes "closer to home" and heightens student interest.

Students extend their analysis of *Animal Farm* to the fifteenth-century allegorical play *Everyman* to identify the symbolism of characters' names and qualities, the conflict between good and evil, and the use of literature to teach morality They then watch a short film clip of Plato's "Allegory of the Cave" and discuss the difference between illusion and reality in the parable and in the novel.

Students end their analysis of *Animal Farm* examining "The Ugly Duckling" and "Snow White and the Seven Dwarfs" for their didactic nature, their symbolism in numbers, colors, and character types, their plot structure, settings, and choices made, and how these contribute to audience expectations for outcomes to fairy tales. Students then assess how *Animal Farm* reinforces or contradicts these audience expectations and discuss how political satire may make for a more effective didactic text than a simple re-telling of political history.

In the second semester, students revisit fairy tales in order to begin an in-depth study of comedy in literature. Good comedy depends on the audience's understanding of the culture in which it is embedded, since comedy's effectiveness lies in its ability to surprise, to show incongruity and contradiction, and to play on an audience's expectations. The audience must have enough background knowledge to "get the joke." The study of comedy, therefore, can be a powerful educational tool since it compels students to understand why something or someone is being laughed at.

As cognitive psychologist Daniel Willingham explains: "Things that create an emotional reaction will be better remembered."[8] And in his "Essay on Comedy," George Meredith said "the test of true comedy is that it shall awaken thoughtful laughter."[9] "Why are we laughing?" then, is a question I ask repeatedly to encourage students to explain their own thought processes. In this way then, comedy is didactic.

After comparing the fairy tale "Cinderella" with Roald Dahl's parody of it, students watch *The Princess Bride* for its parody of fairy tale elements, symbolism, and metaphor and note places in the film where they laugh. They can then discuss how comedy was created by the effect of opposite expectations: what we know fairy tales are "supposed" to be and what we see on the screen.

Because of their dearth of knowledge about quest literature, students study Arthurian legends for their symbolism, heroes, and their expression of idealism, chivalry, and courtly love. They analyze the use of proverbs in quest literature and their didactic role in stories, compare the characteristics of these stories with those of fairy tales and fables, and again connect those characteristics to other stories they have read, in class and on their own.

They revisit parody by comparing chivalry in Arthurian legends, the version of *Don Quixote* in *Man of La Mancha*, and Neil Gaiman's short story "Chivalry," identifying farce, black comedy, and screwball comedy. They also examine insanity and contradiction in Emily Dickinson's poem "Much Madness is Divinest Sense."

They revisit proverbs through the character of Sancho Panza, comparing his "proverbs" with those of Merlin, and compare contradiction and antimetabole (repetition of words in successive clauses but in transposed grammatical order) across texts to understand basic elements of comedy. Allusions are extensively discussed to connect symbolism, quotations, characters, plot sequences, and other literary features in these texts to texts read earlier in the year, in class and on their own.

When they study speeches, they analyze "I Have a Dream" for the rhetorical devices of anaphora, simile, metaphor, alliteration, onomatopoeia, and repetition, and then compare it with the speech by Old Major from *Animal Farm*. This reinforces Carol Jago's idea that, "Metaphorical thinking is not just the province of poets and flakes. It is a life skill. By examining imagery, metaphor, and symbols in . . . literature, students begin to understand how words work their magic on us. It is not just practice for an AP test, it is training for the real world" (p. 16).[10]

Students discuss the inspirational qualities in both speeches and compare their potential for positive propaganda with the negative outcomes and uses of it in *Animal Farm*. Their later study of John F. Kennedy's Inaugural Address and a comparison of it with the character of Don Quixote in *Man of La Mancha* leads to a better understanding of antimetabole, fear, idealism, and "quixoticism."

The year concludes with an intensive study of poetry and music adapted from a lesson by Emily Cobb and Heather Lee at Crowne Pointe Academy in Westminster, Colorado. Because poetry requires more inferences on the part of the reader to fill in "holes," it makes sense to end the year by having students apply the skills they have practiced all year on more difficult texts. With "Jabberwocky," "Sonnet 18" by William Shakespeare, and Polonius's "To thine own self be true" speech from Hamlet serving as anchor pieces, students analyze poetry for tone, mood, and meaning, and compare each piece with popular music and other poetry

Students draw on the elements of comedy and parody they have learned when they write original parodies of "Jabberwocky" and "Sonnet 18," and on rhetorical devices and stances they have learned when they translate Polonius's advice for an instruction book for kindergartners. Both practices help students internalize the elements of these texts; students must understand the underlying concepts completely in order to parody them effectively. Students also analyze the 1987 film *Can't Buy Me Love* for contradictions to Polonius's speech and write a final literary essay comparing the contradictions between the film and the speech.

In conjunction with the texts they read together, students must select and read twenty-five books independently. They keep a list of all books they complete and abandon, and receive credit each quarter for reading the required number. Jago's question is relevant here: "If the only stories students read are ones set in their own time and their own milieu, how will they ever know the rest of the world?"[11] Her question encourages students to "stretch" themselves by reading texts on a college-bound list, especially after reading texts in class by the same authors.

CONCLUDING REMARKS

It may be unethical for teachers to choose not to initiate our students into this country's civic culture by denying them a foundation of historical and cultural knowledge. By reading a sequence of texts that are connected to each other in different ways, and by practicing close reading and learning the connections among these texts, they build bridges across the isolated fragments of their background knowledge for future understandings as literate citizens.

Given how fragmented my students' previous learning experiences were, every year since 2002 I have used culturally and historically significant texts in my literature curriculum to teach the skill sets outlined in Arkansas's standards. Some choices were met with skepticism, with questions from colleagues like "Aren't there newer texts you could use, texts that students might better be able to relate to?"

Today many teachers are lured by an unproven claim that students will engage if the content relates to them. What gets forgotten with the notion that students need literary content relevant to their interests is the broader purpose of teaching literature. And part of this humanistic purpose is helping students to understand the metaphors and other images created by literary works that have influenced later writers and speakers of the language they use.

A student came to me positively vibrating with excitement because he understood not just the literary allusion to "How Mr. Rabbit Was Too Sharp for Mr. Fox" in a sports program about a player being delighted to be back in that "briar patch" but also the extended metaphor. Another student told me that when the narrator of a film on genetics in her science class asked "What kind of brave new world are we creating?" she felt "smart" because she had read *Brave New World*—my suggestion for independent reading after the class had read "Harrison Bergeron"—and understood what the narrator was implying.

Students should understand how the human relationships embodied in the literature they read may be found in their own lives or in the lives of others they know or come to know. But they first have to be able to read that literature. And with a broader and deeper foundational knowledge, students can on their own more quickly make connections among the texts they read, without a teacher's help.

Jamie Highfill teaches English at Woodland Junior High School in Fayetteville, Arkansas, and co-directs the Northwest Arkansas Writing Project. She has published several teaching lessons in Spark the Brain, Ignite the Pen (second edition). Her students are regularly among the highest scorers on the state's standardized tests. In 2011 she was named Arkansas's Outstanding Middle Level Language Arts Teacher.

NOTES

1. E. D. Hirsch, *Cultural Literacy* (Boston: Houghton Mifflin, 1987), xiii.

2. Hirsch, *Cultural Literacy*, 111.

3. Hirsch, *Cultural Literacy*, 112.

4. E. D. Hirsch, *The Knowledge Deficit* (Boston: Houghton Mifflin, 2006), 16.

5. Hirsch, *Cultural Literacy*, 27.

6. Burton Bernstein, *Thurber: A Biography* (New York: Arbor House, 1975), 361n.

7. Henry David Thoreau, "Sunday," in *A Week on the Concord and Merrimack Rivers*, ed. Carl F. Hovde, William Howarth, and Elizabeth Hall Witherell (Princeton: Princeton University Press, 1975).

8. Daniel Willingham, *Why Students Don't Like School* (San Francisco: Jossey-Bass, 2009), 45.

9. George Meredith, "Essay on Comedy and the Uses of the Comic Spirit," *The New Quarterly Magazine*, April 1877.

10. Carol Jago, *Classics in the Classroom* (Portsmouth, NH: Heineman, 2004).

11. Jago, *Classics in the Classroom*, 12.

11

Introducing Close Reading in High School English Classes

Ashley N. Gerhardson and Christian Z. Goering

There has never been an educational context more ready for close reading as the way to approach literary study than now. High school reading scores are stagnant on national tests, and about half of all high school graduates are not ready for college according to American College Testing (ACT).[1] Yet, according to the 2010 national literary survey described in Chapter Two, high school English teachers tend to use nonanalytical approaches for both nonfiction and imaginative literature more than analytical approaches.

The adoption of Common Core's English Language Arts standards by the vast majority of states will change their practices. Their practices will change because these standards and the common tests to be based on them require close, analytical reading. And they do so because it cultivates the habit of reading carefully what is in a text before the reader offers an opinion about what the text means or implies.

The authors of this chapter—Ashley Gerhardson, a teacher of Advanced Placement Language and Composition (APLAC) and AP Lead Teacher, and Christian Goering, a former grade 9 and 11 English teacher and currently a faculty member in a preparation program for English teachers—both faced palpable tensions several years ago when they sought to include more close reading as part of literary study in their classrooms. Their students typically arrived without discernable experience in reading a text closely to determine what the author had actually written or done in a text.

This gap in their students' experience was not surprising. "In recent decades, teachers have emphasized approaches centering on the reader, not the text," Arthur Applebee commented almost two decades ago in his inquiry into the pedagogical approaches used in the teaching of literature.[2] Could reader-centered approaches and text-centered approaches blend together, he asked, given "fundamental differences in criteria for adequacy of response and interpretation?" The tensions had begun in the 1970s as more reader-centered approaches took hold in high school literature classes. Instead of working in conjunction with a text-focused approach like New Criticism—which Ashley and Chris consider the best way to use a reader response approach—many advocates of reader response approaches focused solely on the reader and pushed text-centered approaches out of the classroom.

However, the authors of *Everyday Use: Rhetoric at Work in Reading and Writing*, a textbook designed for and used in APLAC courses, do not believe that text-centered and reader-centered approaches are mutually exclusive or incompatible.[3] They remind us that Louise Rosenblatt in all her work stressed a transaction between readers (and all they bring with them) and texts (and all they offer) in interpreting a text.[4] This was the approach Ashley and Chris brought to close reading in their classrooms. In this chapter, they convey what close reading looked like when they introduced the practice into their classes: one with students who read well above grade level and the other with students who read at grade level or below.

INTRODUCING CLOSE READING IN FORT SMITH, ARKANSAS

The APLAC course concentrates on nonfiction, such as historical documents, speeches, diaries, essays, and articles. The nonfiction readings must be analyzable for rhetorical devices. Although fiction and poetry may be used periodically in this course, they must also be analyzable for rhetorical devices. In Room 3103 at Northside High School, the course begins with a review of such basic literary elements as tone, imagery, diction (connotation and denotation), figurative language, juxtaposition, and antithesis.

Ashley introduced her students to close reading with Jonathan Edwards' sermon "Sinners in the Hands of an Angry God" and some information on Puritan culture. The sermon is in an anthology of American literature and is the first work of nonfiction her students study in it. It illustrates how the elements they studied in fiction function when incorporated into a speech such as a sermon.

After learning about the Puritans' belief in predestination and a wrathful God, the class listened to the sermon on a tape recording by a speaker who sounds like Edwards. Hearing the sermon read in a man's voice, students sensed better its ominous tone. As students listened, one commented: "This is creepy, Ms. G."

Once they had heard the entire sermon, Ashley led her students through the text, breaking apart the sermon line-by-line, paragraph-by-paragraph. During this reading, students were expected to make notes in the margins and in the text. The first paragraph of the sermon is as follows:

> So that, thus it is that natural men are held in the hand of God over the pit of hell; they have deserved the fiery pit, and are already sentenced to it; and God is dreadfully provoked, His anger is as great toward them as to those that are actually suffering the executions of the fierceness of His wrath in hell, and they have done nothing in the least to appease or abate that anger, neither is God in the least bound by any promise to hold them up one moment: The devil is waiting for them, hell is gaping for them, the flames gather and flash about them, and would fain lay hold on them, and swallow them up; the fire pent up in their own hearts is struggling to break out: And they have no interest in any Mediator, there are no means within reach that can be any security to them.

The vocabulary in the first paragraph is quite significant and must be explored first. Ashley listed "natural men," "provoked," "appease," "fain," and "Mediator" on the chalkboard and discussed these words with the class. "What might 'natural men' mean?" One student said "a man who is just himself." Another suggested "one who is saved because the text says they are held in the hand of God." After students offered their ideas, Ashley explained that natural men are those who according to the Puritans are not saved from hell.

Ashley then turned their attention to sentence length and asked: "What do you notice about sentence length in this paragraph?" The students began to look for a period and noticed the combination of semicolons, commas, and colons. One student finally replied: "It is one long sentence." "What might the purpose of such a sentence might be?" Another student remarked: "Could it be to show that this is eternal?" This statement ignited class discussion about the purpose of the long sentence. One student suggested: "It is to show that a decision must be made and that the length of time in hell is permanent and never-ending."

Besides sentence length, Ashley wanted students to understand that parallelism also creates important meaning, as in "The devil is waiting for them, hell is gaping for them, the flames gather and flash about them." Ashley explained that parallelism is the similarity in balance in two or more phrases, such as the arrangement of subjects and verbs. "What kind of tone is created through this parallel structure?" Ashley pointed out some of the key words here: "devil," "hell," "gaping," and "flames" and asked what the last two words convey. "How horrible hell and the devil are in Puritan belief." "He shows the devil as scary and hell as a place to avoid through use of the two words and the driving pace of the syntax."

The final topic of discussion for this paragraph was its figurative language. Ashley asked students to find personification. One student said: "Hell is gaping." Ashley asked: "How does this work as personification?" and "Why would he use personification here?" One student said "Like a mouth. To show Hell's power." "Another example?" Another student responded: "The flames swallow natural men," and continued with "like they can eat like a human."

During this discussion, some students admitted to never having annotated a text before nor really trying to figure out what a text means by reading it slowly and carefully. Their comments were "I can't do this" or "It doesn't make sense," signs of frustration in attempting to read closely. By starting the year with discussion and gradually modeling the process of annotation in discussions, Ashley believes her students became more active readers.

Coming from classrooms where there has been either one interpretation of a text or too many, Ashley found many students at the beginning of an AP course hesitating to go beyond the literal, surface meaning of what they read. However, she knew that they must also learn, among other things, that authors use language for symbolic purposes.

For example, in "The Masque of the Red Death" by Edgar Allan Poe, students should be asked to think about the symbolic significance of the direction of the rooms. When students read the story for the first time, they do not realize that the direction of the rooms may be symbolic of the sun's movement from sunrise to sunset, with sunset, or the end of the day, itself symbolizing the end of life. If they are not asked to notice and think about what an author has done, then their reading is much less rich than it could be.

They should also be asked to think about the symbolic significance of the colors of the rooms in relation to the sun moving from east to west, possibly as stages in life. Below is a passage from this short story about the colors of the rooms and then some dialogue to suggest how this passage can be used to focus attention on the text as well as to stimulate speculation.

But from a certain nameless awe with which the mad assumptions of the mummer had inspired the whole party, there were found none who put forth hand to seize him; so that, unimpeded, he passed within a yard of the prince's person; and while the vast assembly, as if with one impulse, shrank from the centers of the rooms to the walls, he made his way uninterruptedly, but with the same solemn and measured step which had distinguished him from the first, through the blue chamber to the purple—through the purple to the green—through the green to the orange—through this again to the white—and even thence to the violet, ere a decided movement had been made to arrest him.

After reading this section aloud for her students, Ashley asked in what direction the rooms went. A student responded "east to west." Ashley asked: "What does that movement remind you of?" "The sun." "From sunrise to sunset." Ashley asked what sunset may symbolize, especially in the context of this story. "The ending of life." Ashley wrote the colors of the rooms on the chalkboard as she and the students discussed them.

Ashley: "If the rooms are arranged from east to west like the sun's movement, what might the colors of the rooms symbolize? Begin with the first room."

Student: "Blue is first. Could it represent the beginning of life?"

Ashley asks: "Why would you suggest that?"

Student: "Because it is the first room and we dress baby boys in the color blue."

Ashley: "What color is next?"

Class: "Purple."

Ashley: "What might this color mean?"

Student: "Royalty."

Student: "How does that fit into the life cycle?"

Ashley: "Your question of where it fits in the life cycle is excellent. What age do we think our character would be at?"

Student: "In his teens, maybe?"

Student: "Maybe purple represents the time when we make mistakes and learn from bruises?"

Ashley: "Good observation. Can you find any hints in the text about what purple might represent?"

Students: Silence

Ashley: "Which color is next?"

Students: "Green!"

Ashley: "Okay, what might green represent?"

Student: "Grass. Maybe nature."

Student: "He's growing."

Ashley: "Next color?

Students: "Orange!"

Ashley: "What time of day do you see orange?"

Student: "The sunset."

Ashley: "So what time of life might this represent?"

Student: "Getting old."

Student: "Fading away."

Ashley: "Next color?"

Students: "White."

Ashley: "Why might white be placed after orange?"

Student: "White means purity, so that seems odd."

Student: "Ms. Gerhardson, it really doesn't make sense that white would be purity because the people are older."

Student: "I have seen white in movies. You know, Miss. When the character dies."

Ashley: "What might it mean then?"

Student: "Well, that the person may be getting sick and looking back."

Ashley: "Yes, they could be reflecting after their prime. What would that mean?"

Student: "Like when there is nothing else for you to do. You are finished with everything."

Ashley: "Good idea. In color schemes, white represents absence of all color."

Ashley: "Is there anything in the story that gives you a clue?"

Student: "Can't find any."

Ashley: "What is the next color?"

Students: "It's violet."

Ashley: "Good, explain violet to me."

Student: "I'm trying to get it. I know it is right before black."

Ashley: "Then, how might it work in the context of a life cycle?"

Student: "Do you mean like the time before life ends? Violet could be getting dark."

Ashley: "How would people behave in the violet stage of life?"

Student: "They might try to get ready to face dying."

Ashley: "So what's the final color?"

Student: "Black—it's death! It's death!"

For students to learn to read closely, they must be provided with structured lessons first. They need to be asked to think about what words, phrases, signs, colors, sentences, stanzas, and paragraphs in a particular text might mean. Close reading does not necessarily mean that students come to a conclusion or one conclusion about the meaning of a text. They may offer different interpretations so long as they can point to something in the text as support for their particular interpretation.

In most instances, the habit of reading carefully develops when teachers use many kinds of questions to pull students into the text and use texts that lend themselves to close reading. Such texts are multifaceted, multilayered, and thematically complex, with a level of ambiguity that compels readers to go back to different parts of the text, sometimes over and over again.

INTRODUCING CLOSE READING IN TOPEKA, KANSAS

In Room 169 at Washburn Rural High School, Chris passed around printed copies of The Pledge of Allegiance to his grade 11 American Literature class. "While you've seen this text before and have likely said it for a number of years, we are going to read it closely and discuss it in a seminar-style format." Chris wanted students to pose questions to each other about their understanding of the text as well as about the text itself. He didn't want to be the only one asking questions.

Chris discussed the directions for participating in these seminars. His directions indicated that students were to personalize the text by marking down their own reactions in the margins. They could use different colors to mark different ideas. They might also want to think of annotation as having a conversation with the printed words on the page. They could circle words they didn't know, underline key phrases, note word patterns and repetitions or anything that struck them as confusing or important, and write down questions. Chris used this seminar style for introducing close reading to these students because they had had so little experience in earlier grades in looking carefully at what was in a text, which preparing for a discussion about it would require.

Chris led students through their first seminar-style discussion of The Pledge line by line.

Chris: "What do you think about the words used in the first line?" (At first, silence.)

Student: Allegiance is not a word I remember using other than when we say the Pledge.

Student: Interesting point, Sarah. What exactly does allegiance mean?

Student: The dictionary.com entry says that it could mean either loyalty to one's country or loyalty to another person or group. Is that like a marriage?

Chris: Good question Cara, what do you think about that, class?

Student: I don't want to be married to my country.

Student: I agree with you, Steve, me neither.

Student: Wait a second, are you saying that loyalty equals commitment, in a way?

Chris: What exactly do you mean by that, Amber? What does the text say you are pledging allegiance to?

The discussion continued for forty minutes as students grappled with denotative meanings, punctuation issues, and diction. After forty minutes, they had a clearer understanding of what The Pledge of Allegiance means. They also said they wanted more time to prepare for further discussions, something they saw an immediate need for, since all were expected to participate. "We've got to have time to talk to the paper, to really find out what it is telling us, Mr. G," Kelsey offered. "It's like there is so much more to the Pledge than what I thought at first. I've said it over and over but never really considered what it means." In subsequent seminars, students asked increasingly more questions.

This first seminar-style discussion of The Pledge gave students a reason to pay closer attention to textual nuances. Since they are accountable to both their teacher and peers for participation, the activity itself gave them a reason to read and annotate. Students participated in these hour-long discussions every week about texts ranging from historical documents to song lyrics. These text-based discussions over the course of the year gave Chris's mix of regular and special education students many opportunities to learn how to try to understand what they were reading.

CLOSE READING AND THE COMMON CORE

In the introduction to Common Core's English Language Arts standards, a single sentence on close reading indicates a clear shift from educational goalposts of the past: "Students who meet the standards readily undertake the close, attentive reading that is at the heart of understanding and enjoying complex works of literature." This shift is an important one for literary study in America. Instead of only AP students learning how to read closely, all students will be taught how to read analytically. Grade 11 teachers in the future should not have to begin with basic techniques in order to get students to look carefully at a text.

Teacher preparation and professional development programs across the country will need to change to address these new goals. Standards for preparing teachers need to be re-evaluated.

At the University of Arkansas, Chris is working with colleagues in the English department on a course for future English teachers that includes New Criticism among the approaches to literary study they discuss and experience in the course. It is an approach to literary study that has fallen out of vogue in college and university English departments. All prospective literature teachers must be prepared to teach close reading. At present only AP teachers are trained in close reading. Providers of professional development will also need to be trained in close reading.

Common Core's English language arts standards by themselves will do little to change the bleak landscape of students' habits unless the standards are embraced by English and reading teachers. Part of their promise lies in redefining what teachers and students do with a text. In 1915 Sidney Hayes Cox anticipated an ever-changing, challenging world:[5] "We are beginning to realize that the salvation of our republic hangs upon the ability of the ordinary man to think. And he must think more swiftly, deeply, and extensively than ever the forefathers thought" (310).

Nearly a full century later, Ashley and Chris hope that by turning attention to the texts again, but without losing what readers bring to the texts, students will be able to engage more fully with the twenty-first century.

Ashley Gerhardson is the AP English Lead teacher at Northside High School in Fort Smith, Arkansas. Ashley completed her B.S. at the University of Arkansas-Fort Smith and completed her M.Ed. at the University of

Arkansas. She is currently a doctoral student in English education at the University of Arkansas. She is in her fourth year of teaching.

Christian Z. Goering directs the English education program, the Northwest Arkansas Writing Project, and the Center for Children and Youth at the University of Arkansas. Previously, he taught English at the secondary level in Kansas and was recognized as a NCTE High School Teacher of Excellence in 2004 and as a National Board Certified Teacher in 2006. He studies the use of popular music in the teaching of English in middle/ secondary school settings. His work has appeared in the English Journal, Journal of Adolescent and Adult Literacy, American Secondary Education, *and* The NWP Quarterly, *and as chapters in several books.*

NOTES

1. ACT, The Condition of College and Career Readiness 2011 (Iowa City, Iowa: ACT, 2011), http://www.act.org/research/policymakers/cccr11/readiness1 .html.

2. Arthur Applebee, *Literature in the Secondary School: Studies of Curriculum and Instruction in the United States*, Research Report No. 25 (Urbana, IL: National Council of Teachers of English, 1993).

3. Hephzibah Roskelly and David A. Jolliffe, *Everyday Use: Rhetoric at Work in Reading and Writing*, 2nd ed (NY: Longman, 2010).

4. For example, Louise Rosenblatt, *The Reader, the Text, the Poem: The Transactional Theory of the Literary Work* (Carbondale, IL: Southern Illinois University, 1978).

5. Sidney Hayes Cox, "A Plea for More Direct Method in Teaching English," *English Journal*, 1915, 4 (5): 304–310.

12

What Should English Teachers Do?

Fifty years ago, English educators began to implement ideas about curriculum and pedagogy that they believed would be more responsive to lower-achieving students. Their ideas didn't result in higher achievement, however. In fact, students passing through the new curricula with the new pedagogies absorbed less knowledge and acquired fewer skills. The new curricula educators designed didn't work because the premises of these new programs were anti-academic, not to mention ill-adapted to workplace readiness.

This book did not spring like Athena from the brow of Zeus. Rather, it arose from the results of two surveys in 2009. One survey asked over four hundred nationally representative high school English teachers what major titles they assign in standard and honors courses in grades 9, 10, and 11 and how they approach literary study. This survey was conducted by the survey research center at the University of Arkansas. The report on this survey was published as "FORUM 4" by the Association of Literary Scholars, Critics, and Writers in Fall 2010.

The other survey, conducted by a survey research firm in New Hampshire, asked over four hundred representative high school English teachers of standard or honors courses in grades 9, 10, and 11 in Arkansas exactly the same questions. The report on that survey was posted in March 2010 on the University of Arkansas's website.

Both surveys were undertaken to find out what was happening in the English class to the broad middle group of students in our high school.

Were there deficiencies in the literature curriculum and the pedagogical strategies teachers use for literary study that might account for the thirty-year plateau for scores on the high school reading tests given by the National Assessment of Educational Progress? Of particular interest was whether the results of these two surveys would support the thrust of Common Core's English language arts standards, which strongly advocate close reading for both imaginative literature and nonfiction and require increasing complexity in what students are assigned to read through the grades.

The information in the two surveys led to the same three conclusions. First, students in standard or honors courses in grades 9, 10, and 11 experience an idiosyncratic literature curriculum, not a traditional or uniform one. Second, as a class, students do not read texts with increasingly higher reading levels from grade 9 to grade 11. As judged by the use of a readability formula as an objective measure, the average reading level for the major titles taught at each grade level remains about the same from grade 9 to grade 11—and is at about the grade 6 level. Third, teachers more frequently check off using nonanalytical than analytical approaches in the study of both imaginative literature and literary nonfiction.

The second and third results can be regarded as support for Common Core's advocacy of close reading as well as of progressively more complex texts through the grades. However, the incoherent nature of an idiosyncratic literature curriculum is a crucial weakness Common Core does not remedy. Nor was remedy even attempted.

Common Core's standards offer little to aid in the construction of a coherent secondary curriculum for one reason. Its secondary literature standards are mostly repetitious skill sets, that is, slightly differing paraphrases of a basic skill, not culturally rich standards. They therefore cannot guide the development of coherent literature curricula, as can (as one of many possible examples) a former Georgia high school standard such as this one: It required students to "analyze the influence of mythic, traditional, or classical literature on American literature" and relate a work to "primary source documents of its literary period or historical setting" and "seminal ideas of the time in which it is set or the time of its composition."

It is not a professional secret that the secondary literature curriculum in the public schools is incoherent. At the November 2011 conference of the National Council for Teachers of English in Chicago, hundreds of teachers attending a session on national issues in the English language arts openly acknowledged the lack of coherence in their literature curriculum.[1]

Coherence has always been highly desirable in a mathematics, science, or history curriculum. Why not in a literature curriculum, too? Unfortunately, the once coherent literature curriculum most students in public schools experienced until after World War II was first fragmented beginning in the 1960s by changes to the structure of the English curriculum and to the structure of secondary schooling itself.

During these past fifty years, schools have been continuously redesigning their secondary literature curriculum with objectives other than coherence in mind. After breaking up the year-long English course into semester electives to promote students' choice of what they were taught, high schools replaced many older texts in the literature curriculum with contemporary texts on the grounds that they would inspire lower-performing students to read more. They later replaced many older texts with texts by more diverse authors on the grounds that greater diversity in authorship would inspire low-performing students to read. Newly created middle schools did pretty much the same.

However, in both cases, the older texts, which had had, respectively, high school or junior high school reading levels, were usually replaced by easier and often mediocre texts. More challenging and high quality texts by contemporary or diverse authors could have been used.

High schools also encouraged students with poor reading skills to enroll in English classes requiring higher reading levels, presumably to raise teachers' expectations—as if their expectations had been the cause of poor reading skills. Or high schools combined English classes with different levels of difficulty, ostensibly for the same reason but chiefly for social reasons. Easier texts were then used for all students in these mixed or combined classes, even students with grade level reading skills.

Curricula designed to achieve social, not academic, goals inevitably violated the cognitive principles underlying coherence. Social goals weaken and ultimately shatter the coherence of any academic curriculum and eliminate its intellectual benefits. Not surprisingly, there is nothing to suggest that literature curricula redesigned for social purposes produced discernable intellectual benefits for any group of students, regardless of race, ethnicity, or parental income. Reading scores have been mostly flat at the secondary level on NAEP tests since their inception.

Absence of the kind of standards in Common Core that could guide reconstruction of a coherent secondary literature curriculum sparked the major purpose for this book: to spell out principles that undergird development of coherent literature curricula and that at the same time are compatible with Common Core's standards. To do so, it was necessary to pin down what coherence looked like in a year-long or multi-year literature curriculum.

One dictionary defines *coherence* as: "The quality or state of cohering, especially a logical, orderly, and aesthetically consistent relationship of parts." A good working definition for English teachers to use in reconstructing a coherent literature curriculum can be found in the words of Timothy Kanold, superintendent of Adlai Stevenson High School in Lincolnshire, Illinois. "A coherent curriculum effectively organizes and integrates important ideas so students can see how the ideas build on or connect with other ideas, enabling them to develop new understandings and skills."[2]

The attempt to find something useful on coherence in research studies and in articles on curriculum in the English language arts, however, was futile. It was like being on the trail of the Snark, an imaginary creature. But two good examples of coherent literature sequences, created by experienced and well-read teachers, were finally found. An analysis of them suggested the principles undergirding coherence.

These two examples are described in Chapter Nine. One is the grade 6 curriculum in the Brearley School, a private school in Manhattan for academically strong girls. The other is the grade 6 curriculum in the Rainier Scholars program, a private program designed for very able minority students in the Seattle schools. The thinking behind the sequence of titles assigned in either curriculum is independent of tuition, program costs, or the advanced reading skills of these youngsters. Fewer titles could be assigned in a public school for a grade 8 or 9 literature curriculum without damaging the coherence of these two grade 6 curricula.

The purposes for Brearley's grade 6 literature curriculum can easily be discovered by an examination of the titles in it. First, it seeks to familiarize young students with older works that have long been considered culturally significant in this country's literary history and are accessible to them. Second, it seeks to familiarize young students with traditional or classical narratives that served as the major source of allusion or reference in critically acclaimed works of literature com-posed at a later time. Brearley students will read these works in higher grades. Third, it seeks to familiarize young students with works whose language, characters, plots, and events continue to be drawn on for their powerful symbolism or imagery by educated speakers and writers of the English language today.

Moral development is the larger goal for the Rainier Scholars cur-riculum. But it, too, seeks to expose students to the sources of allusion or reference in the many critically acclaimed literary works these students will read in higher grades.

Chapter Nine further shows how the choice of a seminal political docu-ment to address a specific Common Core high school standard can spark a coherent sequence of nonfiction readings from grade 6 on—a form of backmapping. The purpose of this sequence is to enable students to ac-cumulate a body of information they can draw on when they read a pri-mary source document by the time they graduate from an American high school. This example shows how English teachers can make nonfiction texts across grade levels cohere even though they may not cohere with all the imaginative texts also taught at each grade level.

The imaginative texts in this example serve two other purposes. First, they address at each grade another Common Core high school standard, this one requiring study of foundational American literary texts in the eighteenth, nineteenth, and early twentieth centuries. They also show how teachers can gradually foster student understanding of the vocabulary and stylistic challenges of pre-twentieth century American writing across grade levels—by assigning a few eighteenth or nineteenth century texts each year.

While aiming for an informational goal in grades 11/12 from an earlier grade level is a way to create coherence in a sequence of informational titles for interim grade levels, such a goal should not influence everything else read at interim grade levels. It is too narrow a goal to aim for, in contrast to a more open-ended sequence within and across grade levels allowing students to find connections between older works that are impor-tant sources of allusion and reference in the English language and works written in later centuries.

Differences in goals among these curricula can be expressed another way. Both the Brearley and the Rainier Scholars programs aimed for a text worthy of study on its own. In contrast, each of the texts in the sequence leading to a foundational document written in the eighteenth century is unlikely to have a widely-acknowledged cultural significance of its own. The sequence is intended to show coherence over the grades shaped by a relationship in content to a specific informational work with enormous cultural and historical significance.

Nevertheless, the purposes for a particular sequence are not identical to the principles underlying the sequence that create coherence. The categories often used to organize high school courses (genres and literary features) are not identical to these principles. Attention to the principles that seem to undergird the Brearley and Rainier Scholars programs would help English teachers to construct coherent secondary literature curricula that would complement Common Core's skill sets.

OBSTACLES FOR RECONSTRUCTING
CUMULATIVE SEQUENCES IN LITERARY STUDY

Why has it been almost impossible for English teachers who understand the intellectual functions of a coherent curriculum to construct or reconstruct one for literary study? There are several reasons.

Teacher Autonomy

Most English teachers have had and continue to have a great deal of autonomy in what they assign as novels, poems, short stories, and nonfiction texts, whether or not they have a school-selected literature anthology. Autonomy is hard to give up.

Moreover, the secondary English curriculum has for decades consisted chiefly of repeated skills or competencies in language processes (as in two of the three models discussed in Chapter Four). Many teachers have chosen the books they assign knowing that many important skills or competencies could be addressed with any of them. They have also been able to avoid intimidation from professional or higher education sources when they use literary texts that address contemporary political issues or appear relevant to students' daily life or expressions of interest.

Uncriticizable Social Goals

Once social goals led what was considered educational reform, they came to supersede academic goals. The structural changes made to the English curriculum and to the secondary school from the 1960s on would better address the interests of less academically-oriented students or the emotional needs of young adolescents, it was thought. But one social goal led to another.

Electives and middle schools were also used as opportunities to broaden students' social circles. But combining students who had average or above average reading skills with students who had low reading skills, didn't like to read, or didn't do outside reading created an insurmountable problem for literature teachers. A coherent curriculum at the secondary level was not possible in a class with a broad range in reading skills, sometimes from grade 3 to college or graduate level.

To address this range, many secondary English teachers had to include many short literary works with elementary reading levels in their classroom curriculum and exclude long literary works with high school reading levels. It is not surprising that the average readability score at grade 9, 10, and 11 in standard or honors classes in the 2010 national survey as well as in the 2010 Arkansas survey is between fifth and sixth grade. So is the average readability score in Renaissance Learning's 2012 report on the top forty titles students in grades 9–12 say they have read. This is appalling.

Whether driven by the minimum competency testing of the 1980s or the state and federal accountability policies of the 1990s and 2000s, schools knew it was imperative to pay attention or more attention to the academic achievement of their low-achieving students—and rightly so. Teachers were constantly told to try to "meet them where they are."[3] But it was not (and still is not) possible to create one secondary literature curriculum that is coherent and that addresses the academic needs of all students in classes with a wide range of reading skills.

The evidence is not there to support a claim that most students benefit academically from the classroom literature curriculum their English teachers have cobbled together today (even in AP courses). But how many teachers can criticize the dominance of social goals in the literature curriculum?

Non-Cognitively-Oriented Pedagogies

In the absence of a coherent curriculum with clear intellectual goals and content, a variety of noncognitive approaches to literary study could flourish. And they did. Those promoted by the politics of higher education, discussed in Chapter Seven, developed poor reading habits (students cannot summarize or argue about what the author has written) because their goal was celebration of the ego or attitudinal change, not analytical thinking.

Again it is not surprising that teachers of standard and honors courses tended to use a nonanalytical approach to interpret any work (e.g., a personal response or a focus on the work's historical, cultural, or biographical context) rather than to engage students in a careful analysis, or close reading, of the work itself (or at least substantial portions of one). Yes, they may have incorporated some close reading into their mix of approaches to literary study, but they used other strategies most of the time.

For teachers who faithfully followed what Louise Rosenblatt has written, there may not be a contradiction between close reading and a reader response approach if they taught students to read a text closely after an initial response to it in order to arrive at a justifiable interpretation. However, such teachers did not comprise a majority of those replying to the survey. If they did, the survey would have found a better balance between analytical and nonanalytical approaches.

Lack of Academic and Professional Guidance

Perhaps the most important reason why so-minded English teachers haven't been able to reconstruct a coherent curriculum for literary study is that they have received little guidance from higher education on the literary and cultural knowledge they require of incoming freshmen. Nor have they received any guidance from their preparation or continuing development programs on how to construct one.

From Higher Education and State Standards

Our public colleges and universities have long ceased to provide much guidance to high school English teachers about what knowledge of the English language (and the literature that influenced generations of readers and writers of that language) incoming freshmen should have or what reading levels they should have. For example, the University of California's current guidelines for high school course credit expect that entering students "have attained a body of knowledge that will provide breadth and perspective to new, more advanced studies." But it does not provide even general clues to what that body of knowledge is for English language and literature. Far more specific information is provided in David Conley's "Understanding University Success," a monograph showing the kind of knowledge post-secondary English instructors expect of college freshmen.[4]

Similarly, most state standards have not expected high school students to acquire any knowledge of major movements in the history of the literature written in English and of culturally and historically significant works and authors in the English language. The Fordham review of state standards for the English language arts in 2005 found that twenty-five states didn't even mention the existence of a body of American literature (defined however they wished), never mind of British literature, in their English standards.[5]

How could states require students to study historically and culturally significant writers in the English language when they didn't acknowledge the existence of the two major bodies of literature in English? Instead, many states expected students to study "culturally relevant" texts (an indefinable term), as well as "classical and contemporary works from all cultures"—an impossibility for the typical English teacher.

From Professional Sources

There is not even the hint of an admission in the professional literature for English teachers that secondary literature curricula are incoherent. The focus of much of their pedagogical training in recent decades has been on approaches to literary study with noncognitive goals. No prominent educators have dared to claim secondary literature curricula are coherent. But whatever the reasons given for adding specific works to the curriculum (and subtracting others from it), a concern for coherence simply doesn't appear in the professional literature for English teachers.

One can find nothing on the possible negative effects of an incoherent literature curriculum, never mind ideas on how to begin to remedy one. And the major effects are on its overall reading level—and by extension on writing skills, since writing is dependent on reading as both research and experience tell us.

A coherent literature curriculum means having students read some works that were written centuries ago. But works written by dead writers are barely tolerated by education "experts," as we saw in Chapter Four, even in those year-long survey courses in the history of American and British literature (if the latter hasn't been shrunken and buried in a world literature course). Sources of the powerful images that appear naturally in the language of educated speakers and writers (e.g., "salt of the earth") are not covered by the patronizing dictum that teachers should assign texts with "relevance to students' interests" and their "roles in society and the workplace."

Nor can we necessarily rely on education "experts" to advise teachers usefully on the kind of literature they should read to young children. A language arts expert in a school of education told a committee developing standards for Texas that Mother Goose tales are "ethnocentric" and couldn't be mentioned in the standards. Kindergarten teachers who fear ethnocentric children more than illiterate children will keep Humpty-Dumpty out of their classrooms.

To make the situation even worse, the ineffective learning theories and their pedagogical counterparts currently promoted in teacher preparation and professional development programs are also promoted by the National Council for Accreditation of Teacher Education (NCATE). One of its program standards expects prospective English teachers to "engage students in discovering their personal responses to texts and ways to connect such responses to other larger meanings and critical stance."[6]

Only students in Pre-AP and AP classes have been taught to read and write analytically, but nothing has protected students in regular classes from such anti-intellectual expectations. The low level of many college-sponsored summer/fall reading programs, discussed in Chapter One, is testimony to the consequences of such accreditation standards and professionally-encouraged teaching practices.

WHAT TO DO?

First, to address these challenges, secondary English teachers will need to work with more than each other. They will need to work with reading teachers in the elementary and middle grades to construct coherent and progressively more challenging literature curricula for all students, regardless of race, ethnicity, and parental income. And reading teachers will need to learn how to shape their elementary and middle school reading programs so that they contribute to the literary history and literary context for the works assigned in high school English classes.

Second, English teachers must insist that their professional development programs address the teaching of texts rich with allusions and historical references that can contribute to a coherent curriculum. As Thomas Finan, a college and former high school teacher observed: "Close reading and literary history can be complementary helpmates."[7] For over thirty years, both the federal government and state legislatures have handsomely funded professional development programs for teachers and received little in return for their investment.

Third, drastic changes need to be made in the pedagogy as well as the literary content of professional development programs for non-AP English teachers if these programs are to help English teachers to construct and teach a literature curriculum that benefits all the other students intellectually. There is no excuse for a two-track literature curriculum in which only the top 20 percent may read the texts that provide the resources for understanding the language of this country's civic culture. Nor is it social justice to teach only that top 20 percent how to read and write analytically.

As the author of *The Dumbest Generation: How the Digital Age Stupefies Young Americans and Jeopardizes Our Future (Or, Don't Trust Anyone Under 30)* comments,

> We should continue to experiment with educational technology, but we should also preserve a crucial place for unwired, unplugged, and unconnected learning. One hour a day of slow reading with print matter, an occasional research assignment completed without Google—any such practices that slow down and intensify the reading of complex texts will help. The more high school teachers place complex texts on the syllabus and concoct slow, deliberate reading exercises for students to complete, the more they will inculcate the habit....Such practices may do more to boost college readiness than 300 shiny laptops down the hall—and for a fraction of the price.[8]

Fourth, English teachers need to examine carefully the credentials of those who tell them that they should teach only contemporary texts addressing students' presumed interests. How many of the experts who give them guidance on pedagogy have taught literature classes to sixteen-year-olds and can show them evidence of how effective they were? And what about those in charge of developing and reviewing the common test items in English language arts. Are they recognized literary scholars with a broad and deep background in literary studies?

Last but not least, the most important changes secondary English teachers need to make are in their major professional organization. They need to end NCTE's partnership with the International Reading Association, restructure the composition of its executive eommittee to end NCTE's subservience to higher education (both schools of education and college English departments), develop an appropriate set of academic standards for K–12 literature, language, and composition (i.e., disown the 1996 document), and develop an appropriate set of professional standards for the preparation and professional development of secondary English teachers.

CONCLUDING REMARKS

NCTE was founded, its website indicates, "primarily out of protest." At that time, the protest was "against overly-specific college entrance requirements and the effects they were having on high school English education." One hundred years later, secondary English teachers can still protest, this time against the effects of different influences on the high school literature curriculum. Ironically, they would benefit from guidance from higher education on entrance requirements, but this time from the trustees of the colleges and universities their students enroll in.

The discipline-based content that secondary English teachers study still encompasses literary study, language, and composition, as it has for one hundred years. Only experienced and well-read English teachers can make their own professional organization useful to them again and revive a declining individual membership. Only experienced and well-read English teachers can construct coherent literature curricula that initiate all students in our public schools into an English-speaking civic culture.

NOTES

1. Personal observation.

2. Timothy D. Kanold, "'A Common Coherent Curriculum,'" Beyond the Book Leadership Perspectives (Boston: Houghton Mifflin Company, 2011), http://www.beyond-the-book.com/leadership/leadership_082405.html.

3. Sandra Stotsky, Christian Goering, and David Jolliffe, "Literary Study in Grades 9, 10, and 11 in Arkansas." Unpublished report, Department of Education Reform, University of Arkansas, 2010, 33–37. http://coehp.uark.edu/literary_study.pdf.

4. David Conley, "Understanding University Success," report from "Standards for Success," a project of the Association of American Universities and the Pew Charitable Trusts, 2003, 23, section D.

5. Sandra Stotsky, *The State of State English Standards* (Washington, DC: Thomas B. Fordham Institute, 2005), Appendix C, 114–117.

6. These program standards were prepared by the National Council of Teachers of English for the initial preparation of secondary English language arts teachers, grades 7–12 and were approved by NCATE in October 2003.

7. E. Thomas Finan, "Reflection and Tradition: Some Humanistic Observations for Reforming K–12 English Education," paper presented at the 15th Annual Conference of the Association of Literary Scholars, Critics, and Writers, Denver, Colorado, October 10, 2009.

8. Mark Bauerlein, "Too Dumb for Complex Texts?" *Educational Leadership*, February 2011, 68 (5).

About the Author

Sandra Stotsky is Professor of Education Reform at the University of Arkansas and holds the Twenty-First Century Chair in Teacher Quality. She is the editor of *What's at Stake in the K–12 Standards Wars: A Primer for Educational Policy Makers,* published by Peter Lang in 2000, and author of *Losing our Language,* published by Free Press in 1999 and reprinted in paperback by Encounter Books in 2002.

She was senior associate commissioner in the Massachusetts Department of Education in 1999–2003 where she was in charge of revising or developing K–12 standards in all major subjects, teacher licensing regulations, teacher licensure tests, and professional development criteria.

She served on the Validation Committee for the Common Core State Standards Initiative in 2009–2010 and on the National Mathematics Advisory Panel in 2006–2008.

She also served on the Massachusetts Board of Elementary and Secondary Education in 2006–2010. She is now on the Board of Directors of the American Council of Trustees and Alumni.

Among her services to professional organizations, she served as the editor of *Research in the Teaching of English,* the research journal sponsored by the National Council of Teachers of English, from 1991 to 1997. She has taught at the elementary, secondary, undergraduate, and graduate level and published widely on academic and pedagogical issues in a variety of disciplines in the K–12 curriculum.

She received her undergraduate degree in French literature from the University of Michigan. She received her doctoral degree in reading research and reading education from the Harvard Graduate School of Education.